Vibrant Worship with Youth

Vibrant Worship with Youth

Keys for Implementing
From Age to Age: The Challenge of Worship with Adolescents

Saint Mary's Press
Christian Brothers Publications
Winona, Minnesota

General Editor: Brian Singer-Towns

Contributing Authors:

Lisa-Marie Calderone-Stewart	Stephen Petrunak
David Haas	Valerie Shields
Tom Heinen and C. J. Hribal	Thomas N. Tomaszek
Peter M. Kolar	Bishop Kenneth Untener
Michael Novak	Helen Wolf
Sheila O'Connell-Roussell	

Saint Mary's Press thanks the Youth and Worship Committee of the National Federation of Catholic Youth Ministry for its input and guiding work on this resource.

The publishing team included Brian Singer-Towns, development editor; Rebecca Fairbank, copy editor; Lynn Dahdal, production editor; Hollace Storkel, typesetter; Cindi Ramm, art director; Cären Yang, designer; produced by the graphics division of Saint Mary's Press.

Front cover and text illustrations by Michelle Smith. The illustration pictured on the back cover on the cover of *From Age to Age* is by Josef Mahler and is published in *The Image Book: 2,500 Visual and Verbal Images* (Hickory, NC: C. I. Publishing, 1993). Copyright © 1993 by C. I. Publishing. Used by permission.

The acknowledgments continue on page 216.

Copyright © 2000 by Saint Mary's Press, 702 Terrace Heights, Winona, MN 55987-1320. All rights reserved. Permission is granted to reproduce only the materials intended for distribution to the program participants. No other part of this book may be reproduced by any means without the written permission of the publisher.

Printed in the United States of America

Printing: 9 8 7 6 5 4 3 2 1

Year: 2008 07 06 05 04 03 02 01 00

ISBN 0-88489-488-6

Library of Congress Cataloging-in-Publication Data
Vibrant worship with youth: keys for implementing from age to age / Lisa-Marie Calderone-Stewart . . . [et al.].
    p. cm.
  ISBN 0-88489-488-6
  1. Youth in public worship—Catholic Church. 2. Catholic Church—Liturgy.
I. Calderone-Stewart, Lisa-Marie.
    BX1970.23 .V53 1999
    264'.02'00835—dc21   99-050936

 Genuine recycled paper with 10% post-consumer waste.
Printed with soy-based ink.

Contents

Foreword — 7

Preface — 8

Introduction — 10

Youth and Liturgy: There Is Work to Do — 15
   David Haas

Ready to Assemble: Youth as Part of the Liturgical Assembly — 35
   Michael Novak

Fostering Vibrant Worship in Catholic Schools — 47
   Helen Wolf

Active Teens in Liturgical Ministries—It Can Work — 63
   Stephen Petrunak

Spirited Music and Singing — 73
   Thomas N. Tomaszek

Ten Things to Keep in Mind When Preaching to Youth — 87
   Bishop Kenneth Untener

Training Youth for Liturgical Drama — 97
   Sheila O'Connell-Roussell

Vibrant Multicultural Liturgy: Saint Michael's Story — 121
   Tom Heinen and C. J. Hribal

Youth and Liturgy: A Hispanic Perspective — 135
   Peter M. Kolar

Youth and Liturgy: An African American Perspective — 149
   Valerie Shields

Liturgical Catechesis: A Parish Workshop Model — 169
   Lisa-Marie Calderone-Stewart

Appendix: A Checklist for Fostering Vibrant Worship with Youth — 211

Foreword

The writing of *From Age to Age: The Challenge of Worship with Adolescents* was prompted by the belief that gathering for worship is central to the life of all believers. However, many of our young people seem to be missing at the table. Without their presence, we miss the special gifts of enthusiasm and vitality the young church can bring to the larger community.

The 1997 publication of *From Age to Age* prompted ordained, pastoral, and liturgical ministers to gather together with young people to discuss its message. Out of this dialogue came insights, strategies, and a renewed commitment to creating vibrant worship that includes young people. The articles in this manual reflect the fruits of these discussions and will benefit leaders in parishes and schools in their liturgical planning and practice.

Engaging young people in worship is the responsibility of the entire faith community. And there are certainly varied perspectives about the best way to achieve this goal. Therefore, those involved in liturgical, catechetical, family, and youth ministries must see themselves as partners in this noble adventure. I am pleased that the authors of the articles in this manual clearly reflect this collaborative spirit.

May the Lord continue to bless all our efforts in ministry to, with, for, and by young people.

Robert J. McCarty
Executive Director,
National Federation for Catholic Youth Ministry

Preface

To the reader,

Youth are the church of the present as well as the church of the future. If you believe that, then you probably also know that we are not that much different from you adults. We, too, have faith journeys. We, too, struggle to find God in our lives. When liturgy is meaningful and vibrant, it helps strengthen our faith and guide us in our search for God. We'd like to offer the following suggestions that we think would help make liturgy more meaningful and vibrant for young people.

First, help us deepen our understanding of what the Mass and other liturgical celebrations are all about. For example, why do we sprinkle water? Why do we say certain prayers? Why do we stand, sit, and gesture at certain times? Why do we have two or three Bible readings? And how does all this relate to our lives?

Second, make sure young people feel welcomed and involved in your parish or school's liturgies. Liturgy needs to reach out to everyone. If young people are not involved, then the community is not complete. If the parish or school doesn't create an atmosphere that says, "Young people belong here. You are important to us," then youth will not respond in a positive way. Liturgy will be seen as a duty or chore that is not worth our time rather than a desired experience of learning, praying, and celebrating. If we don't develop a love for the liturgy as young people, chances are we won't be attending Mass as adults.

Creating an atmosphere that welcomes teenagers is easy when young people serve as liturgical ministers alongside adults. When we go to church and see other people our age helping out as eucharistic ministers, ministers of hospitality, choir members, servers, and gift bearers, we feel more comfortable participating ourselves. We think, "I'm not the only one here who is doing something."

Third, have teenagers serve on your liturgy planning committees to give input on music, movement, environment, and even homily themes. This will help adult leaders bring a youth perspective into your school or parish liturgies. When we hear a story about young people during a liturgy, we feel included. Our perspective is addressed, and our community reminds us that we are valuable members, not invisible benchwarmers.

To get a better idea of what young people need, adults must ask them. In some parishes or schools, adults decide what youth need and want. This happens not only to youth but also to a lot of other "invisible groups" in the parish or school. The needs and perspectives of African Americans, Hispanics, Asian Americans, Native Americans, women, and people who are disabled, sick, or poor are often overlooked.

The church has made many improvements that encourage a wider spectrum of people to become more involved. What we are saying is, "Keep it up!" If the liturgical celebrations at your parish or school become more youth friendly, usually they also become more everyone friendly. And that is a goal worth working toward!
Sincerely,

Ralph Stewart IV
Stephanie Simic

(Ralph Stewart and Stephanie Simic are on the youth team that helped refine the "Youth-Friendly Liturgy" workshop in this manual.)

Introduction

Perhaps one of the biggest challenges facing the church today is the alienation many young people feel in relation to the liturgy. Though certainly not a new issue, it seems to have reached a new urgency in recent years. In past decades taking a break from liturgical participation often occurred during the college years, but now it seems to be a fairly common high school experience. Indeed many coordinators of youth ministry and directors of religious education express frustration that despite their best efforts, Confirmation is often a "sacrament of departure" from active participation in parish life.

From Age to Age: The Challenge of Worship with Adolescents, published by the National Federation of Catholic Youth Ministry in 1997, is a response to this troubling situation. The paper promotes the continuing renewal of the liturgy. It challenges church leaders to recognize and claim the gifts and charisms of youth. It proposes principles for creating more vibrant worship experiences. And it encourages dioceses and parishes to listen to young people's liturgical concerns and to mentor them in liturgical ministries.

This manual, *Vibrant Worship with Youth: Keys for Implementing From Age to Age,* builds on the foundation laid by *From Age to Age* with further insights and pastoral applications. The articles cover a wide variety of topics, including homilies, involving youth in liturgical ministries, multicultural perspectives, and liturgical drama, music, and catechesis. Among them you will find inspiring success stories, practical approaches and methods, calls to action, and even a workshop outline.

The authors represent leaders in liturgy, youth ministry, pastoral ministry, and campus ministry. Each one contributes his or her unique experience and expertise, making for a rich and delightful mix of perspectives. It is interesting that a common message that comes through in all their perspectives is this: If we celebrate liturgy in ways that are more attractive and meaningful to youth, it will become more attractive and meaningful for the adult community as well.

As you read *Vibrant Worship with Youth,* you may wish to keep a copy of *From Age to Age* close at hand. The articles presume some familiarity with the paper's content and make references to specific paragraphs. The first article, "Youth and Liturgy: There Is Work to Do," provides an introduction to the issues involved and would be a good place to start reading. The other articles do not follow any particular order, so feel free to jump back and forth among them according to your needs or interests.

These articles will serve the concerns of youth and worship only if they lead to continued dialogue and renewal. To foster this dialogue and renewal, consider these possibilities:

- Use some or all the articles with your parish liturgy committee as a basis for discussing and evaluating your parish's liturgical experience. A tool for parish self-evaluation is included in the appendix. Just be sure to include some young voices in your discussion and evaluation.
- Use the articles to continue the dialogue between liturgical and youth ministry leaders in your parish or diocese. The publication of *From Age to Age* contributed to this needed—even if at some times difficult—dialogue. Both groups have found that they have much to learn from each other.
- Use *Vibrant Worship with Youth* as a resource for workshops, courses, and retreats for older teens and young adults. The learning that results will cross both sides of the generational divide.

This is a time of opportunity. Many parishes have already been working hard to make teens feel included and valued in their liturgies. Young people are starting to be trained for liturgical ministries in parishes across the country. National organizations have focused attention on vibrant liturgies that speak to youth. Let us build on this momentum so that the liturgy can truly be our worship, young people and older people joyfully raising our voices together to the glory of God.

A Note About the Illustrations

The illustrations used on the opening page of each article and on the front cover were created by Michelle Smith. Michelle is a young adult from the Diocese of Albany, New York. She created these illustrations as a high school student for a diocesan conference on youth and liturgy. They illustrate the five charisms of youth identified in *From Age to Age: The Challenge of Worship with Adolescents*. It offers the following descriptions of the five charisms.

The Charism of Enthusiasm

The parable of the five wise and five foolish young women (Matt. 25:1–13) provides a contrasting image of both loyal enthusiasm as well as "live for the moment" attitudes among the young. Youth are risk-takers and their energy can be contagious. . . . Their first professions of personal belief are deeply moving to those privileged to hear them. . . . Their enthusiasm supports our taking risks as a community to spread the Gospel.

The Charism of Prophecy

The call of the prophet Jeremiah (Jer. 1:4–10) is often used in prayer services and liturgies with adolescents. Jeremiah, a young man at first fearful to speak God's word, is presented as a model and challenge to youth. . . . Today's adolescents prophesy with their very lives. The danger they face in their struggle to grow up healthy and whole in our "culture of violence" (John Paul II at World Youth Day, *Origins*, vol. 23 [26 Aug. 1993]) is a message for our communities to heed.

The Charism of Service

Mary, the model of Christian service, was a young woman when she was asked to become the mother of Christ (Luke 1:26–38). Her unquestioning "yes" is an example to us all. Today's adolescents are eager to serve and do so in many different settings within and outside parishes. Their charity, compassion, and caring are simple and direct. . . . Their idealism and generosity renew our mission to serve as church.

The Charism of Questioning

In the Jewish tradition, the questions of the young were ritualized (Exod. 12:26). At the Seder, they did not hear these questions as a challenge to the tradition. Rather, the questions were opportunities for the community to retell the story of God's saving acts. . . . Today's adolescents present our parishes with a similar opportunity to retell the story and celebrate the meaning of the liturgy—the paschal mystery.

The Charism of Vision

The disciples gave witness on the day of Pentecost that the Spirit rests upon *all flesh* (Acts 2:17), that is, *all people*. . . . The visions of today's adolescents offer us opportunities to ask "what if" questions about our common life. What if we really lived our worship? The visions of the young challenge us to grow as witnesses of Christ's saving action in our lives.

(*From Age to Age: The Challenge of Worship with Adolescents,* pp. 6–7)

Youth and Liturgy:
There Is Work to Do

David Haas

David Haas is the director of the Emmaus Center for Music, Prayer, and Ministry in Eagan, Minnesota, and campus minister and artist-in-residence at Benilde–St. Margaret's High School in Saint Louis Park, Minnesota. A composer of over thirty collections of original liturgical music, David is active as a speaker, workshop and retreat leader, author, concert performer, and recording artist. He is also the founder and director of Music Ministry Alive!, a national music ministry program for youth and youth leaders.

Those of us involved in ministry with young people continually ask these common questions:
- How do we get young people to appreciate liturgy?
- How do we recruit teenagers to get involved in liturgy?
- What can we do to make the Mass less boring for them?

Sound familiar? In most parishes or schools teens seem disengaged from the worship experience. They are bored or do not even show up at all. They often tell us that the Mass does not speak to them or acknowledge who they are. Youth ministers, liturgists, musicians, catechists, and parents are ready to try almost anything. They either point blame at one another or desperately look for some program or "bag of tricks" to solve the problem.

Let us all give thanks to God for the recent document published by the National Federation for Catholic Youth Ministry *From Age to Age: The Challenge of Worship with Adolescents* (1997). This document is the result of a long-term dialogue between liturgists, catechists, and youth ministers. It helps pave the way for better communication among liturgists, musicians, youth ministers, catechists, and young people themselves. While no single document can offer strategies guaranteed to be successful in all situations, *From Age to Age* offers a fresh challenge to all of us.

The Problem and Challenge

Parents are deeply concerned about their kids not "enjoying" church. In many cases they throw their hands up in total frustration and despair, or they place the responsibility and their hopes for their kids on the parish religious education director, youth minister, or the Catholic high school. But religious educators or youth ministers in the average parish are already burned out with the pastor's and the adult parishioners' expectations. They often feel that the parish liturgical ministers are keeping religious educators and youth ministers at bay. And in many cases, parish liturgists or music directors already feel that they have too much to do; they have no time to take on another task or project. Some believe that involvement in liturgical ministries and planning is more of an "adult" endeavor.

It is not only parish ministers and parents who are concerned about the role of liturgy in relation to teenagers; our young people themselves are deeply concerned as well. At the 1997 National Catholic Youth Convention in Kansas City, Missouri, some three hundred youth told thirty of our U.S. bishops and archbishops that liturgy was their chief concern. Young people from all across the country told them (and the church at large) that they are concerned about the quality of liturgy in their parishes—that it is lifeless and lacking in energy and inspiration; that they feel locked out of the liturgical ministries in most communities; and that they feel they have something to offer the church if only they would be included in the conversation.

In many parishes that I visit today, teens are kept at the edge of parish liturgical life. I do not believe in most cases that this is intentional. Generally teens are encouraged to be involved, but rarely are they intentionally invited into leadership positions. They are not asked for their opinion about music or other discretionary aspects of the liturgy. We want them involved, but it is hard for us to let go of our role.

There are also other reasons for teens' lack of involvement. For example, teens today are much busier than they were decades ago; time commitment is difficult for them. Yet the prevailing problem is that teens often do not feel that the liturgy is for them or that they have been invited to invest in it.

The perceived irrelevance of liturgy to life, and the boredom that many young people express are realities not only for them but for adults as well. The average Catholic who attends Mass every Sunday often experiences the same boredom or apathy toward worship and faith. Perhaps the biggest obstacle to reaching out to young people in terms of worship (and our entire faith life as well) is ourselves, the adult faith community. We often think that young people are different from us. We are constantly searching for approaches to create more "youth-friendly" liturgical celebrations.

I have some strong concerns about this term *youth-friendly* with regard to worship or any other aspect of ministry to young people. First, liturgy and ministry are not about being "friendly." Liturgy and ministry are, however, about being truthful, passionate, and filled with a life-giving proclamation of the Good News. Second, the issue regarding young people and worship is not youth specific; rather, the issue is discovering what is authentic and life-giving to people of *all* ages. If adults approach liturgy with a yawn, then we cannot expect teens to be excited about it either. If there is any difference between youth and adults in terms of how they approach worship, it is that for some reason adults are more willing to accept their boredom. Young people are not as passive in this regard; they will not wait—they vote with their feet.

Some young people also feel that they are being asked to accept our adult agenda, our precepts, our cultural backdrop, our lens on the world.

All our points of view, however good in their intentions, are still being experienced by many young people as hoops they have to jump through. Yes, it is important that our story of faith, our worldview, our wisdom be passed down and shared with young people. Yet we have to balance this with an intentional effort to listen, to wander in their village for a while. Without trying to become an equal in their world, we need to attempt to reverence and honor *their* story, their sacred insight and wisdom. All they are asking is for us to listen, observe, honor, and admire who they are and what they have to offer.

We celebrate "God-with-us" not only in bread and wine, the proclaimed word, and in the presence of the ministers, but also in the community itself, with all its diversity. If we cannot honor the presence of Christ in one another, in all of our humanity, in all of our flaws, in all of our diversity, then we will never be able to fully experience the depth of this presence in our most treasured symbols. Without recognizing the primary sacramental presence of God in human beings, then bread and wine will mean nothing long-term, especially to our young people.

Liturgists and Youth Ministers— Time to Start Working Together

Tackling the daunting task of encouraging young people to become more engaged in the liturgical and sacramental life of the church requires the many diverse gifts that are present in all of us in ministry. The key here is collaboration. The conflict between liturgy, catechesis, and youth ministry has persisted for some time now. Liturgists, youth ministers, and catechists often hold each other in suspicion, judgment, or even ridicule. It is time for this to stop. Each group often believes that it holds the answers to what is good liturgy and what youth need. We often get into heated arguments that actually divide the community and thus our mission. This keeps the parish entrenched in these problems.

My call and challenge to liturgists, musicians, catechists, and youth ministers is this: it is not about *us* —it is about *them*. It is not about liturgical *style* or taste, it is about our young people (and all members of the Christian tribe) being freed and empowered to worship authentically and honestly. It is not about who or what is more important—be it liturgy or catechesis or outreach or youth groups or teen choirs or whatever. It is about whether our young people are truly being evangelized into embracing

Christ as the path for their life. Liturgists and youth ministers need to make intentional efforts to collaborate, to listen to each other, and to discover what our various disciplines and gifts are in order to give to and reach out to each other.

Collaboration is not easy. It is much easier for all of us to do our ministry by ourselves; it is simpler, more efficient, filled with less headaches, and at least in the short run, easier than trying to work with other people. The problem with doing ministry in isolation is that it is not what we are called to as ministers. As ministers we are called to act in partnership with and in openness to the gifts of others. Collaborative ministry helps us to stretch and grow, and in the end, to better serve the needs of our people.

Another difficult aspect of collaboration is that it forces us to truly listen to another point of view, to look at a situation or pastoral problem with another vision or lens. In other words, collaboration requires surrender on our part. We must leave our egos and sensitivities at the door and look beyond to the actual problem. Collaboration requires compromise at times. It holds the value that we do not know everything, that there is always something to learn.

Liturgical Foundations

To forge an effective collaboration between youth and worship in our communities, we need a common language and understanding of worship. Some basic foundational aspects of worship, sacrament, and ritual have to be agreed on and accepted. Without a corrective vision of liturgy, worship becomes reduced to "what we think it should be" or "what we like." I will present five basic fundamentals regarding authentic liturgical celebration that are necessary for effective collaboration among liturgists, catechists, and youth ministers.

1. Liturgy Is a Celebration of Faith

The church did not begin with liturgy and ritual, it began with an intense experience of the person of Jesus. The early church had this experience both with those who knew Jesus personally and, of course, with the post-Pentecostal faith community, the first disciples. Their faith was centered less in the actual historical Jesus and more in the risen Christ. What brought the early believers together was this common experience of Jesus. It was shared among them in lifestyle, service, and worship.

In our culture and church today, worshiping communities have often been formed by geographical location rather than by a common experience of faith. The pattern of Christian identity is often transmitted through attendance at a Catholic school or parish religious education program. Throughout childhood our children are supposed to go to church. It is not an act of choice, rather it is mandated by parents, and they go. Period. This is not the way it was in the early church. Worship and celebration always flowed from faith experience, which was usually communal.

In today's real world of parish life, such faith experience is often hard to find. When our young people tell us that worship is boring, they are not necessarily saying that liturgy is supposed to be "fun," but rather they are longing for a liturgical experience that is passionate. They want preaching that shares and witnesses an experience of God; they want music and symbols that are compelling and take a stand for something other than repetitive routine. They want to hear our stories of how this God has helped us to survive and move forward in our lives. They desire a liturgical experience that is filled with integrity and explodes with energy and ferment. They are not necessarily saying that they want separate youth Masses; rather they are asking that our normative celebrations rise from the ashes of dull routine and become life-giving faith events.

At the cornerstone of faith is the call to evangelize. Worship should celebrate and proclaim regularly an important core of the Good News: there is a God; this Jesus does exist; this God loves us no matter what; we are not alone—a family of people walks the journey with us. Because of this our lives have meaning and hope. If our liturgies could truly celebrate and communicate these wonderful truths, we would have no problem with worship reaching our young people.

When we plan, prepare, and evaluate our liturgical celebrations, the primary question should always be this: How will, or how did, this celebration help those gathered to celebrate, challenge, and confront their faith?

2. Liturgy Is an Action of the Church, Celebrated by the Assembly

Liturgy is not about me, it is about *us*. Liturgy is not a performance by a small group of people to which we observe and respond. Liturgy is an action of the church. As Kierkegaard said: "Worship is like drama. The congregation, they are the actors and the players. The ministers are merely prompters, giving cues and suggestions from the wings. And the audience is God." This wonderful quote should remind us that worship is a communal enterprise in the deepest ancient traditions of our Judeo-Christian biblical faith. In the Hebrew Scriptures, worship is always understood in terms of this relational context. In our Western, U.S. culture, this is a difficult concept. We live in an environment obsessed with individualism, concerned about what "I like," what "I need," and what "my opinion" is. This rugged individualism finds its way into our faith life, and also into liturgy, where everyone has an opinion.

Liturgy is definitely countercultural in this regard. Personal prayer is important and necessary in the spiritual life; however, it is not liturgy. The word *liturgy*, from its Greek roots, means "common work of the people." With this understanding it is not the priest who "says the Mass"; rather it is *we*, the community who celebrate the Eucharist together. The primary minister of music is not the cantor, the choir, the organist, or the instrumentalist; rather it is a musically untrained congregation. They are the primary ministers of sung prayer.

This is an obvious challenge in terms of liturgy with young people. They are in a phase of life that is self-centered and narcissistic in many ways. Again the evaluative question that arises here is: How does this celebration help form them *communally* and help them celebrate their bond with one another as the Body of Christ?

3. Liturgy Is Celebrated Through a Diversity of Ministries

With this understanding of the value of community, worship naturally is a celebration employing the many diverse gifts that exist in every liturgical assembly. These gifts are brought to the forefront in worship in various ways: through liturgical planners, preachers, presiders, lectors, eucharistic ministers, ushers or ministers of hospitality, servers, liturgy committee members, the liturgical environment, liturgical dancers, and, of course, the primary liturgical ministry—that of the assembly itself. Formation, affirmation, and commitment to good catechesis on the central role of the community are important elements for every parish to ponder.

When working with young people, we have to recognize that they possess many gifts, which in most pastoral settings are never truly tapped. Part of the problem lies with some parish and diocesan policies that actually prohibit young people from taking part in these ministries, or the lack of good mentoring of young people in these roles. For instance, young children should be encouraged to participate in the roles of music ministry and lectoring so that they grow up in a church that values and encourages these gifts. When we wonder why young people do not enjoy liturgy, we should ask: How are we involving them in the intrinsic aspects of liturgical celebration?

4. Liturgy Uses a Unique Language of Ritual and Symbol

Liturgy in many ways is purposely an ambiguous action. Although liturgy should be accessible, it should never seem or become fully knowable. This balance between relevancy and mystery is always a hot item for debate among liturgists themselves. This debate carries on between liturgical ministers and people who work with children and youth. It is important to remember that liturgy and its symbols are multivalent in meaning. In other words, in communicating and celebrating the many aspects of our faith, liturgy is to be open-ended, not closed in its intent and purpose.

Liturgy is expressed through the language of symbols, and symbols are at the heart of our Catholic Tradition. The "smells and bells" of our ritual tradition should not be dismissed, except when they are executed mindlessly without any intentional purpose. Imagine a liturgy completely devoid of bread and wine, water, oil, incense, lighted candles, or the cross. What is powerful about these symbols is that none of them, when celebrated well and lavishly, can be reduced to only one solitary message or meaning. Who could declare in one simple declarative sentence what the symbol of the cross means? Who could state in simple language a concrete explanation of the nourishment found in the sharing of bread and wine?

When young people (or anyone else) complain about ritual, they are usually complaining about a ritual experience with no passion, no flair, no energy or investment. Rituals and symbols are all around us—some positive and some negative. Our liturgy needs to hold high symbols and ritual actions that proclaim with boldness the awesome presence and love of God. Quality celebrations are filled with these kinds of strong, bold, and compelling symbols. When we evaluate liturgy, we should not ask, What do these symbols mean? Rather we should ask, Did these symbols and ritual actions evoke some kind of response? Did they provoke deeper thinking and action?

5. Liturgy Is About Mission and Discipleship

Liturgy does not exist for its own sake. Jesus did not come to give us liturgy. Jesus came to activate in us a new way of life and to proclaim hope, reconciliation, peace, and justice. The purpose of liturgy can be summarized in the final words of the liturgy: "Go in peace to love and serve the Lord." The relation of liturgy and justice has always been part of our tradition and is at the cornerstone of our theology as believers. Liturgy celebrates faith but also sends us forth to proclaim and *live* this faith. Liturgy is not an escape, not about having a good time, not about feeling good, or what Sr. Joan Chittister has named a "spiritual Jacuzzi." Liturgy is not therapy, although it has therapeutic aspects. Liturgy is an action designed to provoke a response to live as disciples, as people sent on mission. Liturgy is not about preserving traditional forms in and of themselves, rather it is about proclaiming the real tradition—Jesus Christ—who died, rose, and constantly breaks forth in our midst. The role of worship in our lives is to do more than affirm values or even encourage participation. We must make a commitment to Jesus, to his values, and to one another. In this regard the prophet Amos confronts us and does not mince his words:

> I hate, I despise your festivals,
>> and I take no delight in your solemn assemblies.
> Even though you offer me your burnt offerings.
>
> . . . .
> Take away from me the noise of your songs;
>> I will not listen to the melody of your harps.
> But let justice roll down like waters,
>> and righteousness like an ever-flowing stream.
>>>> (5:21–24)

When we look at our liturgical celebrations through the eyes of our young people, do we see what they see? Often they see a community of people who sing songs and pray prayers and preach sermons about justice, mercy, and loving and reaching out to one another. They see those same people not even talking to one another in the parking lot afterward. We must honestly ask: Do our celebrations evoke a change of life and heart in worshipers? Do they truly transform the community, or are they celebrations of the status quo?

Liturgists and Youth Ministers Working Together: Some Common Principles and Values

If we embrace these foundational constructs of liturgical celebration, then we also need to identify some critical principles and aspects of young people and what they are telling us about their experience of the liturgy. I would suggest six principles, or values, that I believe are essential for an effective collaboration in worshiping with adolescents. Each of these principles cites passages from the Scriptures for spiritual reflection, followed by key quotes found in *From Age to Age*.

1. Young people are full-fledged, equal, yet unique members of the parish worshiping community. They have both a right and a mandate to serve in all the ministries open to adult laypeople.

    Scripture Connections: Gal. 3:26–28; Matt. 25:1–13; Mark 10:14; Rom. 12:4–8; 1 John 2:14

    > As a community, we are less complete when these teens are not with us . . . We are less able to give thanks and glory for the good works God accomplishes through us. (*From Age to Age*, no. 9)

    > Too many parish members are content to describe youth only as the "future church." Young people are members of the church now. (*From Age to Age*, no. 12)

    > We must also challenge distrustful attitudes and procedures that prevent youth from significant parish involvement. (*From Age to Age*, no. 14)

    > Youth, then, challenge the rest of the church not to become settled and sedentary, never to experience itself as fully established or absolutely complete. (*From Age to Age*, no. 28)

    > Adolescents want to give their gifts. . . . We need to make it easier for them to give, particularly in the liturgical ministries. (*From Age to Age*, no. 31)

    > This church today . . . needs the affection and cooperation of her young people, the hope of her future. (Pope John Paul II: World Youth Day Prayer Vigil, August 26, 1993)

The bottom line is that young people want and need to be an integral part of the worship life of the parish. It is not just for their sake; the church needs their presence and gifts. My own story is one example of how a young person was made to feel valued as a true first-class member of the community. When I was a teenager, my home parish did not have a parish music director as many parishes have today. When the musical revolution started to explode after Vatican Council II, our parish, like many other parishes, looked to its young people for participation and leadership. I was one of several talented young people in the parish. I played the guitar and sang, and the parish leadership came to me and figuratively threw me into the deep end of the pool. They said to me, "You play the guitar, you have some talent—*you* lead the music at the Sunday noon Mass."

I had no specific "liturgical formation." I was simply invited by the parish community to offer my gifts. At times we youth musicians did not know what we were doing, and we often made mistakes and bad choices in terms of repertoire. But the point was we were called to be involved and to lead. We picked the music, rehearsed it, led it on Sunday, and though it was not very sophisticated or "liturgically correct" much of the time, people truly responded. We were constantly affirmed, and we filled the church with song and energy. This was not a special teen Mass or anything of the sort. The makeup of the group was young and old, but the musical leadership was the domain of the youth.

Today things look very different in most of our parish communities. We now have full- or part-time music directors or liturgists. On the surface, liturgies have improved in their quality, and the repertoire has become more sophisticated and musically developed. Happily we have learned more about the deep structures of the rites themselves. However, amid these wonderful signs of growth and progress, the youth in many cases are nowhere to be found. The only place where youth are consistently involved in liturgical celebrations is in the Catholic high school, because there they *are* the community. Pastors and liturgists are often critical of school liturgies drawing the students away from the parish. But honestly, why should we be surprised that this is happening? If our parish communities embraced the gifts and ideas of youth, the situation might be different. We need to mainstream young people into the various ministries; we should have young people assisting in preparing liturgies; and most important, we should listen to their ideas and critiques.

It is critical to come to grips with the reality that these young people are part of this church *now;* they are not on training wheels but are full members of the Body of Christ.

2. **Mentoring young people in liturgy, and in liturgical ministries, should be of the highest priority.**

   Scripture Connections: Ps. 78:1–7; Prov. 8:1–21; John 13:12–15

   > Greater youth participation in the liturgy will not occur without an *intentional* effort to seek and encourage it. Parents, pastors, parish priests, youth and youth leaders, liturgy committees, and concerned individuals need to create a local pastoral plan. . . . We need to *intentionally* invite them to participate in our ongoing mission. (*From Age to Age*, no. 12)

   > We must *show an ability to understand their roles and to accept them.* (*From Age to Age*, no. 20)

   > Parents, liturgical leaders, and religious educators need to affirm the talents they observe in youth and provide assistance as teens discern their response to the call of ministry. (*From Age to Age*, no. 21)

   > Youth perceive the experience of parish through their relationship with the pastor and other people who have immediate contact with teens in catechetical or liturgical roles. . . . They develop this perception through one-on-one relationships with significant adults. . . . They are more likely to participate . . . if they have established these personal relationships with the leaders. (*From Age to Age*, no. 37)

   > Pastoral and liturgical leaders need to provide a welcome and safe environment in which teens can offer their gifts and enthusiasm. (*From Age to Age*, no. 84)

   > The foundation of our efforts is our role as youth advocates. (*From Age to Age*, no. 97)

In my experience of working with young people in various settings, I find that when we truly mentor and apprentice young people in ministry, they respond. With gusto! Mentoring is *not* recruiting, which unfortunately is where our strategies tend to be centered, usually with very limited results.

Mentoring is an intentional activity that moves beyond short-term needs—in this case "getting kids involved"—to truly help form and shape a young person's life.

What is a mentor? A mentor is someone who has "been there before" and who establishes a relationship with the novice, providing guidance and a path. First, the mentor is a guide, and second, the mentor is one who is invested in the young person, developing a close relationship with her or him—not a pal or buddy, but one for whom the young person can aspire to or emulate. A mentor is someone who is "irrationally" committed to a young person and her or his success.

A true mentor has the following characteristics:

- is present and available
- is a source of knowledge and, it is hoped, some wisdom
- listens
- provides direction
- helps the young person identify his or her dreams
- is an advocate
- encourages the young person to pursue his or her own dreams
- provides correction when needed
- offers guidance
- is a trusted friend

A mentor is *not* one of the following:

- a parent
- a peer
- God
- perfect

In ministry, of course, the true mentor and model for our life of faith is Jesus. So in the life of faith and ministry, we also help empower young people to rely on the one true source of strength and wisdom: the risen Lord. Mentoring is incarnational theology at its best: through the intentional effort to mentor and apprentice young people, we pass on the missionary message of the Good News. This advocacy is given to us strongly in paragraph 97 of *From Age to Age:* "The foundation of our efforts is our role as youth advocates . . . [who] support families and parishes in providing liturgical formation to the young. We walk with them as they encounter the height and depth, length and breadth of God's love." We are called to share our liturgical and ministerial knowledge, but more important, we are called to share the story of God in our lives and the ways we have experienced the reality of Jesus Christ. We need to love our young people, to be *for* them, to be on their side. Young people today are starving to receive our affirmation and blessing. When was the last time we admired a young person and told her or him so?

3. Youth will only be attracted to a liturgical community that expresses a living witness and experience of faith, using the authentic symbols of its tradition.

Scripture Connections: Deut. 4:5–9

> We trust that the simplicity and tradition of our rites are not in jeopardy when we place our efforts under the guidance of that same Spirit and invite young people to join us in discerning our response. (*From Age to Age*, no. 17)

> The nature of liturgy involves tradition and an expected amount of repetition. Youth can understand this basic dynamic of ritual. . . . As young people become familiar with liturgical rituals and actively involve themselves in the celebration, the church's worship will become more vibrant. (*From Age to Age*, no. 18)

> Most adolescents are not asking for changes in the liturgy. Rather, they look for a basic understanding of the rites so they can more fully participate in the tradition. (*From Age to Age*, no. 24)

> Today's adolescents present our parishes with a similar opportunity to retell the story and celebrate the meaning of the liturgy—the paschal mystery. (*From Age to Age*, no. 30)

I am amazed at the concepts and constructs that young people can grasp. At the Catholic high school where I minister, I am totally in awe of the intelligence and insight that young people possess. Their ability to discern, analyze, and devour complex problems and theories, and to work through and discover strategies, is inspiring. And yet when it comes to church activities, liturgies, prayer services, or retreats, we often feel that we have to "dumb it down" so that they can understand and grasp our sacramental symbols and liturgical imagery.

Young people have a great ability to comprehend our rich liturgical and sacramental tradition, and more important, they are deserving of our efforts to help them do so. We should present our tradition and liturgical richness proudly, not didactically, but with joy, and with all our creative juices flowing. We should not sugarcoat our liturgical rites or be afraid to teach them. We need only take the time to explain the liturgy well and thus give them something to believe in. How can we ask young people to continue to share the story if we continue to keep it from them or are fearful of their acceptance of it? Most young people are not asking us to change the liturgy or to create something new, they just want it to be vibrant and alive.

4. **Nothing can ever be a substitute for the true message of the Good News, namely vibrant preaching and passionate sharing of faith.**

Scripture Connections: Amos 5:21–24 ; Mic. 3:1–5; Luke 1:26–38

> Adolescents assist our faith communities by calling us to the youthfulness and vitality of the Spirit. We do so by expressing ourselves at worship in ways that are appropriate to our own day and age. (*From Age to Age*, no. 16)
>
> Youth grow in faith and appreciation of the power of liturgy to name meaning in their lives when homilists make an intentional effort to preach the Word in a manner teens can also understand and to which they can relate. (*From Age to Age*, no. 22)
>
> Through their honesty and candor, adolescents call us to accountability. Today's adolescents prophesy with their very lives. The danger they face in their struggle to grow up healthy and whole in our "culture of violence" is a message for our communities to heed. (*From Age to Age*, no. 30)
>
> Quality preaching is the number one issue named by youth when they are asked what makes liturgy meaningful. (*From Age to Age*, no. 61)
>
> Today's adolescents are eager to serve and do so in many different settings within and outside parishes. Their charity,

> compassion, and caring are simple and direct. Their lives
> are less complicated by personal needs or agenda than
> adults'. Their idealism and generosity renew our mission
> to serve as church. (*From Age to Age*, no. 30)

Only authentic worship that is consonant with a Gospel lifestyle can witness with integrity. The connection between worship and the church's activity in the world is central to an effective liturgical strategy with youth. Young people need (as we all do) liturgies, music, and preaching that are passionate and take a stand.

All of us deeply desire a worship experience that speaks to our lives. Youth are not interested in specific liturgical policies, dogmas, or doctrines. They are not interested in church politics and controversies, or whether they should embrace all the truths found in *The Catechism of the Catholic Church*. They are, however, thirsting to have a God to believe in and to hear a message of hope, to catch through our passion that believing in this God of ours is worth the effort. They need to hear a message that proclaims a God who is not detached from their everyday lives, and to be reminded that amid the violence, selfishness, and greed of this world, God is always in the mix! Liturgy should be a place where they truly experience a community of people committed to one another—a community who truly surrenders to a power greater than itself and who seeks to live a better life.

I was once with a group of high school students after a powerful all-school prayer service in which we had a guest homilist who was truly on fire. He spoke to them lovingly but at the same time challenged them to be more then they were, calling them to truly commit themselves to changing their lives and following Jesus. It was a simple message, but he delivered it with all the energy and enthusiasm he had in his body. After the prayer service, one of the students came up to me and said, "Boy, if we had homilies like that every week in my parish, I would never want to miss going on Sunday morning." Young people want to be reached, and they are calling us to accountability. Yes, ministering well takes energy, and during and after we may become exhausted. So what? Is it not worth the effort?

5. **Music is an amazing central focus in the everyday lives of young people, as it is also an important normative element in liturgy. In regard to celebration with youth, the role, choice, and implementation of music is critical.**

Scripture Connections: 1 Cor. 9:19–23

> The church has a rich tradition of sacred music, and that has been expanded by the contemporary liturgical music written since the council. Sacred music, by definition, is music old and new that turns our ears and attention to the Creator. . . . We have a responsibility to invite youth to appreciate a variety of traditional and contemporary liturgical music styles. (*From Age to Age*, no. 66)

> The lack of participation has little to do with the music itself. By allowing youth to bring their musical genius to our assembly, we encourage them to value and appreciate the fullness of our sacred musical heritage. (*From Age to Age*, no. 67)

We cannot overestimate the power of music in youth culture, for it is everywhere they are; it is the language central to their culture. Whether we like it or not, music may arguably be the single most influential and formational dynamic in their lives. It was amazing to me on a recent school choir and band tour that just about all the students had a portable CD player with them. They are listening to music constantly. We can choose to sit in judgment of their music, and even reject it, or we can try to understand the culture and environment to which this music speaks.

The topic of liturgical music will be taken up in more detail elsewhere in this manual. One important aspect, however, needs to be addressed here, and that is that young people today do not label religious or sacred music in the same way that adults tend to. Very rarely do I hear young people distinguish between liturgical music, sacred music, contemporary Christian rock, or other songs from the radio. To them, in terms of their faith life, music is music—either they like it or they don't. Either it touches and speaks to them or it doesn't; it doesn't matter if the music is "liturgical" or not.

The effect of music as a formational vehicle cannot be overestimated. Music, and liturgical music in particular, is one of the most subtle and yet effective ways our faith is expressed. How many Catholics could stand up and recite Psalm 91 from memory? Yet how many people could sing all the verses to "On Eagles' Wings" with no music or words in front of them? In other words music is arguably one of the most potent ways our faith is being intrinsically "caught" by our communities. How many people leave the worship space whistling the homily? But the music we sing on Sunday is becoming more and more a part of people's lives both inside and outside the worship experience.

In terms of musical preferences and style, young people are not much different from adults. They have diverse tastes and points of view, more diverse than we can imagine. It is easy (but not accurate) to put their attitudes and tastes, especially in terms of liturgy and music, into a single genre. We often feel we have to provide music that is fast, driving, and in a rock style to reach them. When I talk to students, they say they like all kinds of music: popular, alternative, classical, R and B, jazz, Broadway show tunes; the entire galaxy of musical genres is present in their preferences. We must honor and affirm young people's ability to transcend a particular style or piety. Their tastes are as diverse as adults'.

However, musical style cannot be seen as the definitive issue. More important, it is the inclusion of youth and their gifts for music making that the church must recognize and revere. Young people want to be involved as music makers themselves. They *love* to *make* music. At events and liturgies where the young people themselves are the leaders, the response is amazing. We need more recorded and published resources from liturgical music publishers that feature young people as the singers, instrumentalists, and composers.

6. Good authentic liturgical celebration implies and requires an intergenerational experience.

Scripture Connections: Exod. 12:26; Deut. 4:9–10; Jer. 1:4–10; Joel 2:28–29

> Teens want to belong. They want to feel welcomed. They are very sensitive to the hospitality displayed at liturgy. (*From Age to Age*, no. 72)

> Youth who tend to isolate themselves in their peer groups need to be challenged to experience also the family's and community's expression of prayer. (*From Age to Age*, no. 73)

> Youth want to be included in the conversation. . . . They also want their issues to be given due consideration. Liturgical leaders should not be troubled when teens question

> the reasoning behind some liturgical practices. (*From Age to Age*, no. 77)
>
> **Sunday mass is the prayer of the whole Body of Christ, and, therefore, the assembly should never be limited to one age group or another.** (*From Age to Age*, no. 93)

From Age to Age is very pointed and determined in its vision that liturgy is never a celebration of an isolated age, gender, or cultural group. Liturgy is always, without exception, a celebration of the *entire* Body of Christ. We need to remember that to be Catholic means, "Here comes everybody!" We live in an age in which people shop for a parish and for liturgy the same way they shop for a car or for other material goods. Far too often people look for a parish of people who look alike, think alike, act alike, and share similar views on matters of the world and faith. This "cafeteria Catholicism," though understandable, is not an authentic vision of what faith life is all about. The table of God's word and meal is for all, regardless of age, gender, skin color, political preference, economic status, sexual orientation, or cultural or ethnic background. Our liturgical celebrations must be for all.

Teen liturgies and other experiences set aside from the normative Sunday parish eucharistic celebration are increasingly taking root in many parishes. This is certainly understandable, and in many cases these experiences have arguably been "successful." Many movements, such as LIFE-TEEN and other programs, have been effective in reaching young people who feel locked out or isolated. However, I believe that this is the wrong solution to the right problem. I certainly understand the frustration of youth ministers and teens who feel that Sunday Mass is boring and out of touch with their lives. But when we create separate celebrations, we create a more divided community. Separating the Body of Christ into age or other specific groups of people is not a healthy manifestation of community.

In talking to young people, I find that many of them are desperately longing to be a part of the Sunday celebration, to help lead the music, to serve as lectors, eucharistic ministers, and ministers of hospitality. They would like to be involved in the planning of parish celebrations alongside adult members of the community. Although being a part of a teen choir can be fun for them, they also want to be part of the regular adult music ensembles and groups. We have to remember that they do not want to stay teenagers but to grow into adulthood and into the adult world and adult activities.

The solution, in my opinion, lies not in creating separate weekly experiences for young people (although certainly there is nothing wrong with occasional celebrations just for youth at retreat gatherings and other events), but in taking a hard look at our regular Sunday liturgies. Here are some questions that we need to ask ourselves:

- How are we including the gifts of young people in leadership ministries?
- How are we involving young people in the planning and preparation of liturgy?
- Are young people on our parish liturgy committees?
- Do we ever invite them to offer their reflections and evaluations of the quality of our liturgical life?
- How are we mentoring them in liturgy?
- Are we reaching out to them?
- Are we inviting them to come with us to liturgy workshops and liturgical music conferences?

From Age to Age challenges us to invite teens to be involved in order to create liturgical celebrations that speak to their lives.

The Next Step

The task before us is difficult. Many liturgists, musicians, presiders, and homilists feel unqualified to speak to the needs of young people. Some youth ministers and catechists feel that the present liturgical structures, symbols, and patterns are not relevant, or are inadequate to speak to teenagers. All that most young people are asking for is some passion, some care, and some willingness to be heard. They want and need a liturgy to provide them with signs, smells, sounds, and stories that give them hope and proclaim a vision of how to survive in this world. Liturgy can accomplish this. If we are true and authentic, God will always be faithful. We do not have to create new rituals; however, we do need to breathe new life into them. We need to rediscover the power and potential of ritual, and believe in the power of God (who really is in charge).

Our young people are capable, willing, gifted, and ready to serve. They are waiting, waiting for us. So let's give it a try—let's get together, listen, learn from one another, and work together for our youth. They are certainly worth the effort.

Ready to Assemble:

Youth as Part of the Liturgical Assembly

Michael Novak

Michael Novak is the director of the prayer and worship office for the Archdiocese of Milwaukee and a member of the national board of directors for the Federation of Diocesan Liturgical Commissions. He has worked professionally in the field of liturgy and liturgical music for more than twenty years.

Not all youth possess the charisms to be liturgical ministers, but all youth need formation to understand the ministry of the assembly. (*From Age to Age*, no. 53)

The Primary Ministry of the Liturgical Assembly

Imagine that you are at a child's birthday party. Everyone is seated around the room, the presents have been opened, and a lighthearted spirit fills the air. Now the time has come to serve the cake. The lights are dimmed, but no one leaves their place to go to the dinner table, where the cake will be served. As the candle-crowned cake is carried in, there is stillness. Some of the guests make halfhearted attempts at the birthday song, but a kind of murmuring is all that is heard. When the cake is brought to the table, the guest of honor blows out the candles perfunctorily, and there is no applause or laughter. Another birthday has been celebrated.

In the United States at the end of the twentieth century, that is not how most people expect children's birthday parties to unfold. It is presumed that everyone will gather around the table, sing the birthday song, and laugh and clap when the candles are blown out. The very form of the celebration as we have come to know it demands that everyone participate—the more noisily and off-key the better! Any attempts to change the song or to keep the guests away from the table or to otherwise alter the routine are viewed as quirky at best, and some might still insist on doing it the way they know anyway. The logic of our birthday ritual demands that all participate and that everyone be included; otherwise it is not a birthday party.

Similarly, the logic of our liturgical rituals demands that all participate, that all be actively engaged in the actions and the prayers. Such active participation by the people has not always been emphasized in the long history of our church, but with the Second Vatican Council, our precious heritage has been reclaimed. The first document produced by the Council, *The Constitution on the Sacred Liturgy* (*Sacrosanctum Concilium*, 1963), tells us:

> The Church earnestly desires that all the faithful be led to that full, conscious, and active participation in liturgical celebrations called for by the very nature of the liturgy. Such participation by the Christian people as "a chosen race, a royal priesthood, a holy nation, God's own people" (1 Pt 2:9; see 2:4–5) is their right and duty by reason of their baptism. In the reform and promotion of

the liturgy, this full and active participation by all the people is the aim to be considered before all else. (No. 14)

In the *General Instruction of the Roman Missal* (the "user's manual" for the Sacramentary), we read, "The Church desires this kind of participation, [and] *the nature of the celebration demands it"* (no. 3, emphasis added). In other words, we cannot really call it a Mass without the people's active participation, any more than we can call the previous example a birthday party.

Although it is not my intention to trivialize the Mass by comparing it to a birthday party, I want to make absolutely clear from the outset how indispensable the assembly's role is in the celebration of the Eucharist. In this article I will explore conditions that work against the primacy of the assembly, examine some reasons behind those conditions, and offer some strategies for a fresh approach.

As we begin, a few terms should be defined. The word *assembly* has a precise meaning when used to describe the community that gathers for a liturgical celebration. It refers to *everyone* who has come to worship, including all the ministers and even the priest. In this way it differs from the term *congregation,* which is often used to refer only to the "people in the pews," or the word *audience,* which has no place in describing the liturgical action of the faithful. I will also use the word *ministry* to refer to the work of various specialized liturgical ministers such as lectors, cantors, ushers, greeters, altar servers, communion ministers, and so on. I would like to stress again that the ministry of the liturgical assembly is primary, and these other ministers can perform their roles only because they are, first of all, members of the assembly.

Finally, the primacy of the assembly can only be properly understood in the context of God's invitation to us. It is God who convenes us in Christ, as members of Christ's Body. The actions the assembly performs at the eucharistic celebration are performed with and through Christ, who calls us to unity with him in offering the sacrifice of praise.

Conditions Working Against the Primary Ministry of the Liturgical Assembly

In the ideal world, the principle of the primacy of the liturgical assembly would be supported by the way each and every parish worships. But we live in the real world, and a number of conditions may undercut that principle.

From physical barriers to psychological ones, these conditions affect the worship of everyone, including youth. Presented here is a description of some of the major experiences or conditions that work against the assembly's ministry. In the section that follows this one, I will suggest reasons why these conditions are frequently allowed to continue.

The Worship Space

When we enter our churches, many of us find ourselves in a physical environment not unlike a theater, with the sanctuary at one end of the room and all the pews facing the same direction. Our natural tendency in this environment is to equate the sanctuary with a theater's stage and to slip into the role of audience, even when the liturgy invites us to be the performers. Because of the architectural forms we have inherited, even our buildings and furnishings may undercut the principles of active participation and the primacy of the assembly. Rather than a people performing an action that takes place in our midst, we tend to become an audience that watches a drama unfold on a stage before us.

Pre–Vatican Council II Habits

Habit is another obstacle to realizing the ministry of the assembly. Even now, thirty years after the liturgical reforms, some parishes have not integrated the spirit of *The Constitution on the Sacred Liturgy* into all aspects of their worship. And so singing may be minimal or performed almost exclusively by the choir or soloists; speed and efficiency may be valued more highly than full, engaging symbols; the presence and gifts of differing populations (such as young people) within the parish may go unacknowledged. Habits born of practices carried over from another era, habits rooted in a lack of attention to the demands of the rite, or habits that spring from a failure to recognize the needs of the community all work against the ministry of the assembly.

Poor Examples in School, Catechetical, and Youth Programs

Liturgical practices at elementary schools and the primary grades of religious education programs may present their own challenges. The main role of the ministry of the assembly is betrayed when we hear teachers and catechists say, "We wanted everyone to participate, so we put five children in the gift procession and prepared eight to read the petitions." Specialized liturgical ministry is thus confused with the primary ministry of the assembly, to the detriment of both.

When liturgies for children are so completely different from their Sunday experience, older children and youth get the idea that liturgy is only "kid stuff" that they are ready to grow out of. Often childish songs and cutesy performances or activities imposed on children's liturgical celebrations create a strong distaste for liturgy in early adolescents, who see themselves as growing too sophisticated for "Hi, God" and hand puppets. Because these experiences of children's liturgy are so completely different from the Sunday experience, many young adolescents can't make the leap from children's liturgy to Sunday liturgy and so may reject all liturgy as irrelevant.

The way some liturgies are celebrated with youth may also diminish the role of the assembly. In some cases the priest may preside in such a way as to focus attention on himself and how well he can relate to youth. This heightens the role of the presider at the expense of the role of the assembly. In other situations poorly prepared young people are pressed into service as lectors, musicians, or other ministers, and their efforts, however valiant, distract and diminish the prayer of the assembly.

Understanding the Reasons Behind the Experience

In the previous section, I listed some experiences that work against the primary ministry of the assembly. Before we can explore strategies for supporting the ministry of the assembly, we need to uncover some of the reasons that these conditions persist. Understanding these reasons may help lead to a sound approach to overcoming the obstacles they present. Usually the situation is less the result of a lack of goodwill than it is a lack of good information.

The Entertainment Paradigm

A serious challenge to the task that liturgy sets before us is the entertainment mentality that pervades our culture. We are trained from birth to be passive consumers of whatever the sports and entertainment worlds offer us. Increasingly, athletic activities and performance arts are being left to a highly skilled few while the rest of us watch and listen. Further, the advent of personal electronic equipment means that more and more of us can passively watch in our own private space without interacting with others.

As we lose the habits of singing, speaking, and moving in communal groups, our liturgies become more and more countercultural. We have begun to use our cultural paradigms to interpret what we do in church rather than the other way around. That is why when the physical structure of the church resembles a theater, we automatically become an audience rather than an assembly. What happens to our liturgies when we come expecting to be entertained and to have everything done for us? What happens to the power of our liturgies to shape and mold us in the Christian life if we cease to move, sing, and speak together with any conviction?

Misunderstanding Full, Conscious, and Active Participation

Often members of the assembly lack understanding about the meaning of full, conscious, and active participation. Some do not realize that it is "the aim to be considered before all else" (*Constitution on the Sacred Liturgy*, no. 14), and so they keep doing things the way they always have. The result of this is the parish in which pre–Vatican Council II habits persist. Others who may have a passing familiarity with the term *active participation* may think it means that everybody has to do everything all the time: if you're not singing or responding out loud, you're not participating. The outcome of this approach is liturgies that are "busy" and don't allow needed quiet time for introspection and reflection, which are vital parts of the assembly's full and conscious participation. This tendency to latch on to a liturgical principle in an unreflective way is often the reason behind habits of inattention to the real demands of the rite or to the needs of the community.

Desire to Foster "Involvement"

Well-meaning people who equate specialized liturgical ministries with participation may do more to hurt the cause of the ministry of the assembly than anything else. The idea that you're not really participating unless you have something special to do is a prevalent one; ask almost any teen about their ministry, and you'll hear something like, "I wanted to participate, so I became a lector." This idea is reinforced in special youth liturgies that assign every person a liturgical ministry so that everyone is "involved."

The motivation is not at issue here; anything positive that attracts someone to a liturgical ministry is a cause for celebration. The problem is the attitude that it conveys: being part of the assembly means that you're not participating, that you've got nothing important to do. This is the exact opposite of the principle that states that the liturgical assembly is the primary actor in the liturgical celebration.

Parish-Based Strategies for Supporting the Role of the Liturgical Assembly

More than one observer has noted that most of the principles espoused in *From Age to Age* could apply equally well to liturgy with people of any age. This is also true of the ministry of the assembly—the issue of the assembly's role is present at all parish liturgies, not just at liturgies with young people. Knowing this has consequences for how to approach the issue in the parish. One cannot devise strategies for supporting the role of the assembly only at liturgies for youth. Doing so would cause at least two problems: the liturgies with youth would be separated from the mainstream of parish life, and the young people would be disappointed and disillusioned any time they attended the other parish liturgies.

Learning how to support the role of youth as assembly necessarily involves a comprehensive approach that addresses the role of the assembly at every parish celebration. So as you consider the strategies I suggest here, you will find they will affect not just youth participation positively, but the whole parish community.

Formation

Because understanding the primacy of the liturgical assembly is basic to supporting it, formation must be an important ingredient of any strategy. In particular the parish staff and leadership must all share the same approach to supporting the assembly's role so that they are able to sustain one another and work together to move the parish in the same direction.

Formation for Pastoral Staff

The first group that must be on board with a clear understanding of the role of the assembly at liturgy is the pastoral staff. As a staff they should take time to study and discuss the appropriate sections of the liturgy documents and even take a field trip to a nearby parish where the assembly's role is already well supported. The diocesan worship office can provide materials and guidance, and may also be able to provide a facilitator for the process. Who should be included in this in-service? The pastor and any priests who regularly preside at liturgies at the parish, religious education staff members, youth ministers, the school principal, liturgists and staff musicians, social-justice or human concerns ministers, pastoral associates, and deacons. It may also be wise to include support staff so that they will be able to handle questions that may arise from any new practices as a result of the in-service.

Formation for Schoolteachers and Catechists

Another important group to bring on board is schoolteachers and catechists. They are on the front lines of the formation for children and youth, so they must understand and support any efforts to enhance the assembly's role at worship. They, too, would benefit from an in-service or evening of training (depending on their schedule).

Formation for Liturgical Ministers

All the parish liturgical ministers need to learn how what they do affects the assembly. For example, cantors should be aware that singing every song into the microphone might actually discourage participation in the singing. Although such information should be a part of their regular formation sessions, special meetings may be appropriate if changes in their routines are involved. Always be sure to explain what they are doing and why. As a means of catechizing the parish leadership, it may also be useful to invite parish council and committee members to formation sessions for liturgical ministers, even if they don't undertake a ministry themselves.

Formation for the Parish at Large

Although liturgy has its own power to catechize and form the community, parishioners can also be given information about the assembly's role in the liturgy through a variety of means: bulletin articles and inserts, newsletter articles, and good, strong liturgical preaching, educational sessions, and workshops, to name a few.

Intermediate Steps

Situations may arise in which in-services are difficult to arrange. Yet even if all the pieces aren't in place, some things can be done. The youth minister could request to be put on the agenda of the worship committee meeting to ask for support in developing the role of the assembly through new practices and training of liturgical ministers. Religious education catechists could still be trained even if the schoolteachers aren't. If a diocesan office isn't available to help, there are good written resources available on the role of the assembly. (I recommend *Celebration: Theology, Ministry, and Practice,* Oregon Catholic Press's collection of Rev. Eugene Walsh's works.) Adopting a piecemeal approach isn't the ideal, but with determination and creativity, much can be done.

Preparing Parish Liturgical Celebrations That Empower the Assembly

Keeping the ministry of the assembly foremost in the minds of planners and ministers may be a new challenge; some may even call it a paradigm shift from old ways of doing things. The things planners should consider range from the simple to the profound: from making sure that everyone who enters the church knows which worship aid to use and where to find any music they might need, to planning rites like Baptisms that include plenty of responses for the assembly and the possibility even of some movement.

At some point members of the parish liturgy committee should review each liturgical policy and practice to see if it promotes the assembly's role and to look for ways to improve it. For example, too many parishes allow the assembly to sit during the Communion procession. Try having everyone stand and sing throughout all of Communion, as the rubrics tell us to. It makes a marvelous difference in the assembly's sense of being involved in a unified action.

Celebrations with Youth

While the worship committee is developing practices that support the role of the assembly for the whole parish, some things also may be done whenever youth gather to worship, either on their own or as part of larger parish celebrations. Consider the following suggestions when preparing for liturgical celebrations with young people.

Processions

As I mentioned earlier, one of the biggest psychological barriers we have to deal with is created by the physical space of our churches, where a sanctuary set up at one end or side of the room creates a "stage" and an "audience." If this is your situation, try to make sure that more of the action happens amid the assembly and requires the physical involvement of the assembly. Processions are a good example. At a recent parish celebration of the stations of the cross, rather than having everyone remain seated in the church while a few ministers moved from station to station, all the youth present were involved in the movement around the church.

In the Rite of Christian Initiation of Adults, the Rite of Acceptance calls for the entire assembly to go outside the church and bring the candidates inside. If the assembly is too large or if space is too confining for the whole assembly to go out to greet the inquirers, make advance arrangements with a group of parishioners, including young people, to go out to greet them.

Better Use of Liturgical Space

Investigate the possibility of rearranging the space. Can at least the ambo be moved into the midst of the assembly? For a small gathering, can everyone fit into the sanctuary? For evening prayer can chairs be brought in and arranged antiphonally (facing each other) at the front of the church even if the pews all face the sanctuary? One caution: don't invite people into the sanctuary during the eucharistic prayer unless there is enough room for everyone. Think of what it says to the liturgical assembly when only some are invited to gather around the altar.

Homily and Presider Preparation

Have the preachers invite young people to be part of their weekly homily preparation sessions with parishioners. In addition to the homily, presiders should incorporate the experience of parish teens sensitively into other prayers of the Mass. The idea here is not to draw attention to how "with it" the priest is, but to help the youth members of the assembly feel included in the actions and prayers of the parish. It is hoped that the priest is similarly inclusive of other members of the assembly as well.

Acknowledge Youth Activities in Prayers and Rituals

Prom blessings, graduation blessings, inclusion of youth events in general intercessions, and mention of youth concerns in the intercessory section of the eucharistic prayer are some suggestions for creating an atmosphere of inclusion that says that the presence of the young people in the assembly is important to the parish.

Youth as Liturgical Ministers

Inviting young people to serve in every parish Mass as liturgical ministers will have a positive effect on the self-perception of their peers as members of the assembly. Those who do perform such ministries should have the necessary skills and should satisfy the same training requirements as all the other parish liturgical ministers. Serious liturgical ministry does not allow for last-minute drafting and on-the-spot training. To do otherwise is to show a lack of respect for the liturgical assembly.

Formation for Youth

Not every liturgy need be a Eucharist, and young people do need to gather on their own as well as being part of the parish Sunday celebrations. When the young people gather for prayer outside of Sunday Mass, follow good principles of engaging and supporting the assembly's prayer in the planning and celebration. Then engage in some mystagogical reflection (that is, talk with one another afterward about what you did, why you did it, and how you felt).

Further Considerations

Other articles in this book offer suggestions for creating vibrant and engaging liturgy for youth. Following those suggestions at all parish liturgies will give young people a strong sense that they belong not only as members of the parish's liturgical assembly but also as a significant part of parish life.

In developing a parish attitude of support for the role of the assembly, in general it is better to stay away from gimmicks and fads. Especially with youth, adopting solid practices at eucharistic celebrations, which can transfer into their adult experiences of worship, will be more beneficial in the long run. For times when the youth gather on their own in noneucharistic settings, such things as liturgical drama and dance may give expression to another important side of their spirituality that will nourish them as well.

The approaches in this article can each be thought of as responding to either the conditions that work against the ministry of the assembly or the reasons behind those conditions. As you seek to develop your own strategies for fostering liturgies that are engaging, especially for youth, keep a critical eye open for the obstacles in your parish and try to uncover the reasons behind them. When you can address the reasons, the obstacles are more easily overcome.

Why All the Fuss?

When all is said and done, one might still ask why it is so important to place all this stress on the central role of the assembly. The answer is a simple one: If we truly believe that our liturgy shapes us, forms us, and nourishes us for the Christian life, then we absolutely must have an assembly that is strong and active. If our liturgies do little more than allow us to be idle recipients, what kind of Christians will that make us?

Forming our young people to appreciate their role as members of the liturgical assembly may help them to understand that as members of the Body of Christ they have an obligation to do more than sit passively in a pew on Sunday morning. They can bring an energy and vitality to our assemblies and thus to our parishes if we give them a chance to get in the habit. They come ready to assemble as the church of today as well as the church of tomorrow. Let's give them every chance we can!

Fostering Vibrant Worship in Catholic Schools

Helen Wolf

Helen Wolf has been teaching for thirteen years in the Diocese of Brooklyn, New York, and has been a liturgical musician for over twenty years. Currently she teaches religion and social studies at Bishop Loughlin Memorial High School. Helen is a facilitator for "The Catholic High School as Faith Community" workshops sponsored by Saint Mary's Press.

Great things are happening in Catholic schools because the Spirit is alive and working in our midst! But when religious educators and campus ministers try to get this across to students, we are often confronted with looks of puzzlement. That's because saying it isn't enough. Young people need experiences that enable them to recognize and celebrate God's presence in their lives and in the world. That is why good liturgy is one of the greatest gifts that Catholic schools can offer young people. By definition the liturgy is a time of profound prayer when we recognize and celebrate Christ's presence.

There is a growing tendency among Catholic schools to have fewer liturgies rather than more, which is a cause for concern. Our belief that Christ is present in the Eucharist in a real, substantive manner is a core belief of the Catholic faith. Celebration of the Eucharist should be central to the life of the Catholic school. "The liturgy is the summit toward which the activity of the Church is directed; it is also the font from which all her power flows" (*Catechism of the Catholic Church,* no. 1074).

When understood and properly celebrated, the liturgy can become a powerful, vibrant form of prayer for students living in a time when communal ritual and prayer is difficult and, for some, alien. Leaders in Catholic schools are discovering that for school liturgies to become vibrant experiences of prayer, some important principles must be followed. In this article I'll explain these principles and then describe some specific strategies for implementing them.

Guiding Principles

Teach the Liturgy

Young people's understanding of sacramental symbols and rituals is often limited and unformed. Even students raised in the Catholic faith may not know what's going on when the priest elevates the bread and wine. A 1997 study carried out in the Diocese of Rochester, New York, revealed much confusion about Holy Communion. Of those questioned in eight parishes, 60 to 65 percent did not believe Christ was present in the Eucharist (Strong, "Catholics Are Confused on the Meaning of Eucharist," pp. 1, 5). This study paralleled a *New York Times*–CBS News poll conducted in 1994. We cannot expect young people to find the Eucharist a fruitful form of prayer unless they understand what's going on. No wonder *From Age to Age* emphasizes that "the fullness of the Church's sacramental life—the sacraments of initiation, healing, and life mission—should be the subject of intentional catechesis for youth" (no. 38).

Our students have many misconceptions and questions about the Catholic faith: "Why do Catholics worship statues?" "Can't Catholics be considered cannibals for eating the body of Christ?" "Why are Catholics baptized as infants?" These questions and others can be discussed and clarified in a liturgy course, dispelling stereotypes and creating a clearer understanding between Catholics and non-Catholics about their respective faiths.

Catholic schools across the country have found their enrolments of students from other faith traditions increasing in recent years. Liturgical catechesis provides a wonderful opportunity to share our Catholic faith. The liturgy is a phenomenal tool for catechesis in and of itself! By sharing the beauty and history of our liturgy, many students, both Catholics and those of other faiths, come to a much deeper appreciation of the richness of Catholicism.

If your school does not have a liturgy course, and implementation of one is not on the horizon, start on a smaller scale. For example, a week before the first school liturgy is celebrated, you might review certain core aspects of the liturgy with your students in classes already in progress. Perhaps a component on the liturgy can be added to existing religion courses.

Recognize All Members of the School Community

The function of Catholic schools is to promote the spirit of the Gospel in the daily lives of all present. Yet this can be a daunting task given the diversity of schools in the United States today. Think about all the members of the school: students, teachers, administrators, secretaries, custodians, the nurse, cafeteria staff, parents, alumni, and the board of directors. Then there are the subgroups: jocks, artists, bookworms, ethnic cliques, club members, extroverts, and introverts. Finally, think of the different cultural backgrounds they come from: European, African, Hispanic, Native American, Asian, and all their subgroups. It's difficult working with vast differences in the classroom when the numbers are small. Imagine the anxiety when hundreds of students and other members of the school community are gathered together in one place—to pray! Can one form of prayer engage all these distinct people? YES!

The liturgy is our opportunity to share our faith in community with the whole school population. For the liturgy to be a vibrant experience for all assembled, though, it must acknowledge the diversity of its members and pull from the traditions and practices of the community. *The Catechism* saw the need to address the diversity of the church in this era:

> The celebration of the liturgy, therefore, should correspond to the genius and culture of the different peoples. In order that the mystery of Christ be "made known to all the nations" . . . it must be proclaimed, celebrated, and lived in all cultures in such a way that they themselves are not abolished by it, but redeemed and fulfilled. (No. 1204)

The solutions aren't easy, but a good place to start is by making all feel welcome. A spirit of hospitality must be present when your faith community sits down together to pray. Think about what hospitality means when entertaining houseguests. It refers to food, shelter, and a welcoming environment. This means committing your time and energy to making your guests feel welcome. We must do the same for the members of our school faith communities. Once the students, faculty, staff, and other members present at the liturgy are welcomed, the way is clear for the work of the Holy Spirit. The school is providing an opportunity for all to listen freely for the movement of God's spirit in our lives.

Make the Liturgy Central

Celebration of the Eucharist is central to the life of the Catholic school. But many Catholic schools are opting to celebrate special days with prayer services instead of Mass. This is due in part to the diversity of religious faiths in our school communities, as well as to the difficulty of securing a priest to preside at Mass. What does the decision to have fewer liturgies do to the faith development of our students? Will it lead to a generic nurturing of the students' relationship with Christ, at the expense of our Catholic identity? There is no easy answer to these questions, and schools need to struggle with them. One thing is certain, though: if Catholic Christianity is to be cultivated, the liturgy must continue to be a significant form of school prayer.

Many schools have made a commitment to continue celebrating the liturgy frequently. They plan liturgies for holy days of obligation, celebrations of the liturgical seasons, and the feast of the school's patron saint. Special liturgies can also be planned for incidents unique to the school community, such as the death of a student, milestones in students' academic careers (graduation, ring ceremony, etc.), and faculty days. Not all these need to be celebrated with eucharistic liturgies; a mix of eucharistic liturgies and special prayer services allows for variety and creativity.

I believe, however, that using worship to celebrate all areas of a school's life is an important way to build faith community within the school. Celebrate the work of students and faculty performing acts of community service. Have an optional lunchtime Mass once a week. (Students find this especially attractive during Advent, Christmas, Lent, and Easter.) Bring athletic clubs to the liturgy before or after big events. The varsity basketball players in prayer on the gym floor can serve as great role models for other students.

Nurture graduates by offering the liturgy at reunion celebrations and alumni gatherings throughout the year. Solicit ideas from them regarding their needs for prayer—even asking some of them to serve on the liturgy committee.

Perhaps most important of all, a very special liturgy should be celebrated to mark the beginning and end of the school year. It's crucial that the entire faith community gather together in prayer at these times to set a spiritual tone and focus for that academic year and for their lives.

Prepare Well for Liturgical Celebrations

Liturgies must be dynamic and engaging. This will not happen without deliberate, thoughtful preparation. The formation of a liturgy committee is essential. Because the liturgy should reflect the lives of the various members of the community, the liturgy committee should include youth and adults who reflect the varying perspectives and needs of the school's population. Study your school's breakdown of gender, ethnicity, and religious affiliation, and try to have at least one person on the team representing each of your school's major populations. Even with the best intentions, a white male campus minister may not understand Native American tribal rites, and teachers can't always determine what kind of music adolescents find uplifting.

This brings us to the next point: the liturgy committee must include students. The majority of any school faith community is the student body. How can they not be represented when planning prayer for them? Students who are part of the planning process have a vested interest in making the liturgy significant to them and their classmates. Their participation on the liturgy committee will help them explore and recognize more clearly the presence and activity of God in their lives and in the world—an evangelizing act.

I believe one of the liturgy committee's most important jobs is to schedule liturgical celebrations well in advance, similar to the way other events are planned in the high school. The rest of the planning will follow once your calendar is set. It was a chaotic time for the liturgy committee at Bishop Loughlin in our first year because we didn't schedule our prayer services and liturgies at least a year in advance. Each month we ended up trying to plan for the next few weeks. When we moved to planning a year in advance, we solved several problems:

- Specific dates were selected, and the prayer services and liturgies were printed on the school calendar. This helped convey that worship is an integral part of the life of the high school faith community.
- The dates on the calendar helped some faculty who were frustrated because of lost class time. Once the services were on the calendar, teachers were able to structure their classes more efficiently.
- We were able to secure commitments from committee members to facilitate the planning of specific services. In this way all the work did not fall on the campus minister for every service.
- The ministers for the services—celebrant, choir, song leaders, altar servers, lectors, liturgical dancers—had more time for preparation. This was an important factor, especially for the directors of the choir and dance groups in planning rehearsal time.

Another critical role for the liturgy committee is to reflect on and periodically evaluate the community's liturgical experience. The committee's self-evaluation is important, but just as important is a school-wide assessment. This could take many forms—anything from a five-minute discussion in classes to a written evaluation that faculty, staff, and students complete. See the resource at the end of this article, "Liturgy Evaluation Form," for one simple example. These evaluations will serve as a guide to planning more effective liturgies in the future.

Specific Strategies

Don't fall into the trap that what worked for us when we were kids will necessarily work for students today. A rule of thumb for creating vibrant worship in Catholic schools is, "Don't be afraid to be innovative." Suggest any idea to the liturgy committee. One reason for having so many diverse members involved in the planning phase is to bounce ideas around and weed out those that won't work. It's amazing how many effective ideas typically come out of those discussions!

Of course anything you do as part of a sacramental liturgy must be consistent with the church's liturgical principles and guidelines. But within those guidelines there is room for creativity, flexibility, and cultural adaptation. The following are specific strategies Catholic schools can implement to make the liturgy more dynamic and spirited.

Prepare a Sacred Space

We enter holy ground when we gather for the liturgy, but often our sacred space is the same area used for last week's basketball game. If you use a space for the liturgy that is used for other non-liturgical functions, look for alternatives, like a local church. If that's impossible, students must be told that the space is to be considered holy. Ask them to walk in silently so that others may pray undisturbed. Have someone greet them at the door, reminding them to be respectful of others' prayer time. The liturgy begins as students walk into the sacred space, not when the priest approaches the altar.

Trying to "dress up" a gymnasium for prayer is like trying to get an elephant through a needle's eye, but some nuances may help. Use any available lighting, like directing spotlights to accentuate the altar and dimming the rest of the lights. Bring in plants, flowers, and banners. Arrange chairs so that the congregation is close to the altar. Have music playing softly in the background to set a quiet, prayerful mood. Consider burning incense to quiet the senses.

One aside—if all these measures still don't set the mood and someone must address students regarding their behavior, this person should be someone other than the presider. The presider's goal is to keep the space spiritual and prayerful. You don't want the person leading your students in prayer to discipline them before the entrance procession.

Focus on a Theme

Developing a theme for each liturgy is an excellent way to plan. The theme should emerge from the Scripture readings of the liturgy of the word. Be aware that the lectionary contains readings for special liturgies, too, which you can use for special occasions.

The liturgy's theme helps focus your planning and unifies all parts of the liturgy: the entrance processional, music selections, the homily, and the prayer of the faithful. A blueprint, if you will, takes shape.

To come up with a theme, begin by reflecting on the Scripture readings for the liturgy. What theme or issue emerges from them? Then look for connections between the scriptural theme and the students' personal lives, experiences, and concerns. It is amazing how often the scriptural themes easily tie into the issues of young people: relationships, peer acceptance, violence, drug addiction, alcoholism, abortion, and even death. When the liturgy addresses these concerns, it makes the experience relevant for young people. Whenever possible, be sure to involve young people in this reflection process on the liturgy theme. It can be quite an eye-opening experience.

Use Music That Appeals to Youth

Good music is essential. I've had the most success using the students' music. "One Sweet Day," by Boyz II Men and Mariah Carey, is powerful for an All Souls' Mass, as is Kirk Franklin's "Lean on Me" for AIDS Awareness Masses. Look to the students as your living resource of information. If music is needed, tell them the theme, and they will inevitably find contemporary music that is spiritual and fitting. That's not to say that traditional music has no place in the high school setting. Bishop Loughlin's one-hundred member choir moves freely between Vivaldi's "Gloria," Haugen's "Mass of Creation," and "Siahamba," a traditional South African hymn—and all are received well by the students.

Try incorporating a mix of ethnic music. A blend of Franklin's "My Life Is in Your Hands" with "Pescador de Hombres," along with a Jamaican rendition of the Lord's Prayer may seem like a crazy mix, but it sings to the heart of a faith community made up of African American, Latino, and Caribbean American peoples.

Who should lead song—one person or a choir? This varies according to a number of factors, including how formal the liturgy is, the number in the congregation, even the size of your sacred space. The key is to engage the congregation in song. This is perhaps the most daunting challenge for a music minister at a high school liturgy! Having the words available for the congregation is a step in this direction. I don't like handing out song sheets to hundreds of students for many practical reasons, so I type the lyrics on a transparency and display them on a large screen during the Mass. In any case don't be afraid to try a variety of music styles and methods to engage the young people in song. It's from this variety that you will find what works best with your congregation.

Remember Paul's words when your students are not as enthusiastic as you'd wish: "Be filled with the Spirit, as you sing psalms and hymns and spiritual songs among yourselves, singing and making melody to the Lord in your hearts, giving thanks to God the Father at all times and for everything in the name of our Lord Jesus Christ" (Eph. 5:18–20).

Use Homily Time Effectively

Liturgies in a Catholic school setting provide a unique opportunity for opening God's word to young people. Because the homilist isn't facing an intergenerational audience, he can truly focus on young people's issues and life experiences. And if the homilist is also the chaplain of the school, he is in a wonderful position to connect stories and examples from the life of the school to the Scriptures' themes.

But what happens when the priest or deacon is not accustomed to speaking to teenagers? I hope this is not the case with your school's chaplains, but many schools without chaplains must bring in priests from the community for regular or special school liturgies. With great tact and discretion, you may need to prepare the priest or deacon for giving a youth-friendly homily. Being born and raised in Brooklyn, tact does not come naturally to me, but one good way of attempting this is to have the presider meet with a group of students before the liturgy. Together they can reflect on the liturgy's readings, and the students can share with the homilist their stories and experiences that connect to the readings' themes. You can also share with the homilist the article in this book "Ten Things to Keep in Mind When Preaching to Youth," by Bishop Kenneth Untener.

A technique many schools have found useful in liturgies with small groups is the dialogue homily. During the dialogue homily, the presider gives some opening remarks and then asks the congregation to share their insights and stories. This is an almost certain way of securing the conscious and active participation of young people. An opportunity to ask questions and offer personal viewpoints is very engaging, especially if your students are accustomed to the traditional homily of sitting and listening—not a young person's favorite activity.

The homilist's words, however, are not the only words through which God speaks. Consider asking other members of your faith community to give personal reflections after Communion, as a Communion meditation. Invite the most popular teacher *outside* the religion department to share a personal story of forgiveness during a Lenten liturgy. Imagine the physical education teacher sharing a faith story with students who have only seen him in sweats and in the gym! Students need to see that faith is a human experience, not the religion department's domain. Still more dynamic would be to ask a so-called bad kid to give witness from his or her life. So often teens are falsely labeled and stereotyped by peers and adults. Wouldn't this be a great way to see other people for who they are, not for how they dress or for the type of music they enjoy?

Do not overlook the people in your faith community who are performing great acts of charity outside the school. Their stories would make excellent reflections. Ponder this: Who in your school do people know very little about and may want to get to know this upcoming semester? Ask these individuals if they would be willing to share their faith stories. Try tapping your alumni to share their life experiences as well. The results of your research may astound you!

Include Students from Other Faiths

In keeping with the need to make all feel welcome, each school must address the sensitive issue of who receives Holy Communion. Most Catholic schools have growing enrollments of students and staff from other faith traditions. Nothing is more anticlimactic and unwelcoming than asking them not to receive the Eucharist after spending forty-five minutes in prayer together.

To avoid awkward and embarrassing moments at the Communion table, focus on this issue at the beginning of the year in a catechetical setting. The catechist can address this issue by looking at it from the viewpoint of the teens' and their families' beliefs. Students and faculty from other faith traditions might not want to violate their beliefs about Communion or publicly proclaim a unity with the Catholic church that isn't there. The religion classroom, rather than the liturgy space, is the more appropriate place to address this issue so that students can engage in a dialogue with the teacher.

To preserve an atmosphere of hospitality during the eucharistic celebration itself, many schools encourage everyone to come to the altar in the spirit of community prayer. Those who are not Catholic can receive a blessing or share a moment of prayer. How well this works depends on how the congregation is prepared and taught about the Catholic belief in the Eucharist. And whatever you do, don't ask for a show of hands to see who is Catholic in order to count out the hosts! Students from other faiths find this very alienating. We must trust that when given the facts of our traditions and beliefs, they will respect the differences in doctrine.

Make Room for Students' Prayers

"By prayer of petition we express awareness of our relationship with God" (*Catechism,* no. 2629). When our students offer prayers for their families, friends, and personal needs, they are turning to the Creator for divine grace. Students crave God's saving love, perhaps more so today than ever before. We must give them opportunities to voice their intentions, and the prayers of the faithful during the liturgy can help fulfill this need.

Too often one person writes the prayers of the faithful, and the prayers fail to reflect the diverse needs and concerns of all present. The liturgy committee, representing the diversity of the school community, should help ensure that the prayers of the faithful (within reason) reflect the needs and concerns of all those gathered. Using prayers the students write themselves is always a good idea. Challenge them to integrate current events, the needs of the faith community, and the needs of the world. "Teens need opportunities and encouragement to voice spontaneous prayers . . . and bring their ideas and issues to community prayer" (*From Age to Age,* no. 59).

Finally, when possible, present the opportunity for spontaneous offerings to allow for the needs not expressed in the prepared petitions. The heavens rejoice when we turn to the Lord in prayer. We must offer our students every opportunity to join in building the Kingdom through shared prayer.

More Strategies

The previous strategies were important "big picture" things to keep in mind for preparing vibrant school liturgies. Now here is an assortment of other, less critical strategies that can also enhance the students' worship experience:

- If using any written programs, italicize written explanations of the parts of the Mass. The explanations will serve as reminders to the congregation as to what is to happen at different points in the liturgy.
- Integrate a variety of cultural symbols into your liturgies. For instance, incorporate Kwanzaa principles into a Christmas liturgy, or a Mass on the feast of Epiphany for the Latino

students. You can solicit these ideas from a diverse liturgy planning committee or by consulting with others in your larger community. Several articles in this manual contain ideas for multicultural inclusiveness.
- Expose students to other forms of Catholic prayer, like exposition of the Blessed Sacrament, recitation of the rosary, Gregorian chant, the stations of the cross, and novenas. Herein lies the history of our church. What a great opportunity for a deeper understanding of the beliefs of Catholicism. We must help our students respect and reverence different forms of prayer.
- Students' lives are filled with chaos and noise. When exposed to guided meditations, they are enabled to slow down and pray, not just with words, but with their entire beings. A guided meditation can be a powerful way to deliver a homily. We have used guided meditations successfully in our liturgies, and the young people always remember them. Remember: offer many different types of prayer experiences to the many different types of students in your school. You don't know what will work for which student.
- Tie in coursework as prayer during the liturgy. Art classes studying Van Gogh can give a visual sermon following the parable of the sower with Van Gogh's painting called *The Sower*.
- Explore the Internet. There are numerous Web sites for Catholic educators. Ideas and questions can be batted around in the chat rooms and list servers with religion teachers and campus ministers across the country. See the "Suggested Internet Resources" section at the end of this article for some web sites I've found helpful.
- Look through your texts and manuals for prayers, guided meditations, and liturgy themes. Teachers' manuals seem to be the forgotten resource, usually because they're so voluminous and intimidating. The extra effort may produce some valuable ideas.
- You may want to use real bread for Communion. Wafers don't look like the kind of bread our students are used to, and bread could add a new dimension to their understanding of the

Eucharist. There are several good recipes available for making bread that conforms to liturgical requirements.
- A healing Mass can be very appealing for a variety of needs, especially regarding violence in society. Have a candlelit procession to begin a Mass for a victim of violent crime. A healing Mass could encompass many other needs, such as war, abortion, alcoholism, and child abuse.

Some Final Thoughts

The work of building vibrant worship in Catholic schools can seem like an overwhelming challenge, but be at peace. The Spirit is already at work in your school. See the steps you take to enhance prayer as a nourishing of the grace already present among your staff and students. It is God's work; it doesn't all rely on your efforts!

Start small. Undertake one task at a time, but if nothing else, form a liturgy planning committee. It is from this core representative group that your liturgies can take flight. Make sure the young people are involved. Let them take responsibility for nurturing their relationship with God. If it's new and innovative ideas you're looking for, the young people are your best library and most valuable treasure.

Your success in creating dynamic liturgies must include your administration and the celebrant. Get them on board with all your plans, drawing from their phenomenal academic, spiritual, and life experiences. And for the written word, look to the *Catechism of the Catholic Church,* the church's liturgical documents, and the other articles in this manual for encouragement and ideas. Explore all your resources—living and written—to build better liturgy, and the Lord will be pleased!

My final thought is to encourage you to take time to nurture your own spirituality. I leave you with the inspiration of the patron saint of teachers, John Baptist de La Salle, founder of the Christian Brothers. During the early eighteenth century, De La Salle struggled to educate poor and disadvantaged boys in France. Even though he wrote three hundred years ago, De La Salle's words echo true for Catholic educators today:

> You must . . . devote yourself very much to prayer in order to succeed in your ministry. You must constantly represent the needs of your [students] to Jesus Christ, explaining to him the difficulties

you have experienced in guiding them. Jesus Christ, seeing that you regard him as the one who can do everything . . . and yourself as an instrument that ought to be moved only by him, will not fail to grant you what you ask of him. (*Meditations*, p. 439)

Suggested Internet Resources

- *www.smp.org/hs*. Saint Mary's Press's Web site has a special section for high school teachers called Faith Community Builders. It includes discussion forums (including one on school liturgies), resource articles, links to other sites, and more.
- *www.fas.harvard.edu/~pluralsm/html/about.html*. This is a link to the Pluralism Project, Harvard University's study of the growing religious diversity in the United States, with a special view toward new immigrant religious communities. Lots of links.
- *www.bu.edu/sth/BTI/ecudocs/etiquett.html*. This site is an excellent resource on interfaith etiquette.
- *www.ncea.org*. Gateway to the National Catholic Educational Association.
- *www.catholic-church.org/dioceses/usa.html*. Links to many diocesan sites.
- *www.mcgill.pvt.k12.al.us/jerryd/cathmob.html*. An excellent compilation of links by a Catholic high school theology teacher.

Liturgy Evaluation Form

The religion and campus ministry departments, in the hope of developing better liturgical experiences, need your opinion for future planning. To assist us in meeting your spiritual needs, please take a few minutes to complete this form and return it to the campus ministry department mailbox this week. Thank you for your time.

Liturgical celebration being evaluated: _____

Date: _____

1. What did you like most?

   _____
   _____
   _____

2. What did you like least?

   _____
   _____
   _____

3. On a scale of 1 to 10 (10 being the highest), rate the following aspects of the liturgy:

   _____ entrance procession

   _____ Scripture readings

   _____ homily

   _____ prayer of the faithful

   _____ music

   _____ atmosphere or environment

Resource A: Permission to reproduce this resource for program use is granted.

Liturgy Evaluation Form 2

4. Did you feel welcome and comfortable as a member of the assembly?

   (circle one)   Yes   No   Somewhat

   Comments:

   _____

   _____

5. Would you like to take an active leadership role in a future liturgy?

   (circle one)   Yes   No   Somewhat

   If yes or somewhat, how?

   _____

   _____

6. Did the theme of the liturgy relate to your life?

   (circle one)   Yes   No   Somewhat

   Comments:

   _____

   _____

7. Do you have any suggestions or ideas for future liturgy themes?

   _____

   _____

8. Other comments:

   _____

   _____

   _____

   _____

Active Teens in Liturgical Ministries—

It Can Work

Stephen Petrunak

Stephen Petrunak is the music director at Saint Blasé Parish in Sterling Heights, Michigan. Stephen is also a professional musician; he teaches guitar, has written guitar instruction manuals, and gives music workshops nationally.

Five years ago, during only my second full month as music director at Saint Blasé, the mother of an eleven-year-old child named Zack approached me regarding his playing violin for a wedding liturgy. I was a bit taken aback by Zack's age, and drew the conclusion that this was probably not a very good idea. Unless he was a child prodigy, certainly Zack could not possibly be ready to play violin during a wedding. At the urging of the bride, I decided to at least hear Zack play his violin. Imagine my amazement as I listened to this child play so expressively and beautifully, nothing close to what I had imagined. Within thirty seconds my musical impression of Zack drastically changed. I promptly informed his mother that he would be more than welcome to join the other adult musicians at the wedding.

As I further questioned Zack's mom about his musical experience, she shared with me that they were members of a nearby Catholic church in which the music director refused to allow Zack to play his violin at the liturgy. The reason? Zack was told he was too young, and was not given the opportunity to share his incredible giftedness. I immediately informed his mom of our music program at Saint Blasé, and added that our adult contemporary music ministry, which provided music for worship every week, would love to have Zack play his violin with them. Zack began sharing his musical talent with our community the very next week, playing his violin in a music ministry in which the average age of its members exceeded thirty. Five years later, at age sixteen, Zack has blossomed into an unbelievable musician whom I consider a musical peer. He has provided a wonderful role model for all the young people of our community.

Several months after Zack's arrival, members of the music program were invited to gather for a brainstorming session. One of the goals that emerged was to start a teen music ministry in our parish. This idea came from a long-standing member of the music program, who also volunteered to direct the new ministry. At the time our community had been blessed with an active children's choir, but the vast majority of these children stopped singing around the seventh grade, never again finding their way back into music ministry. We agreed that if the parish had a teen choir, we would have a greater chance of keeping youth involved in music ministry when they became adults. That year we began the Teens Loving Christ (TLC) music ministry, which over twenty teenagers immediately joined.

It was not but three months after the start of the TLC ministry that another parent, this time the father of a twelve-year-old girl, asked if his daughter could come and practice playing the organ at our church just once a week. I learned that Linda had already played organ at her own church, and also had studied piano for a number of years. The request seemed simple enough, so I offered her the use of the organ any weekday afternoon. When I heard Linda play for the first time, I asked her if she knew that we had a teen choir at Saint Blasé and if she would be interested in joining this newly formed ministry. Within three months Linda was playing piano and organ with our TLC music ministry. Just six months after meeting Linda, I began working with her as an accompanist for our weekend liturgies. Linda is now one of the most dependable, committed, and effective accompanists we have at Saint Blasé. All the cantors love working with her. She has recently shared her desire to one day become a full-time music director.

Was it mere coincidence that Linda stumbled into our community? What opportunity would have been lost if I had never listened to Zack play? It is now five years since I became director of music at Saint Blasé, and during this time teen involvement in music ministry has blossomed. Consider the following examples:

- The TLC ministry currently has about twenty-eight members who minister at any given weekend liturgy. They are integrated within the community—they minister to the elderly as well as the young.
- Although some music leaders claim that teens must have their own liturgy at which to minister, our teens share their musical gifts with the entire community. They even use most of the same music selections that the other music groups use, including the "dreaded" traditional hymns.
- For the past three years, TLC has provided the music for the Confirmation liturgies (a way for teens to minister to teens). Two of our teens are currently active as cantors and also minister at the different weekend liturgies.
- Zack and David, another incredibly talented fifteen-year-old guitarist, recently organized a musical benefit concert to provide our community with social-justice awareness and support the American Red Cross. They handled virtually all the details of this concert, with only minor adult supervision.
- A thirteen-year-old cello player named Scott occasionally plays with one of two existing contemporary adult music ministries within the parish.

My experience in music ministry and with teens affirms my belief that teens do not need to be separated from the parish community to become active in liturgical ministries. Rather teens have become a central part of our music program because they feel needed and wanted and because they have been given the chance. Why do the teens in our music program feel needed and wanted? I believe five elements promoted teen involvement at Saint Blasé: strong parish leadership that values teen partnership in ministry, a vision for teen participation, visible youth role models, encouraging and supportive mentors, and a parish community that accepts teen involvement. These elements have sent the message loud and clear to all Saint Blasé young people that they have a ministry in the church—ultimately the church belongs to them as much as it does to the adults.

Five Principles for Promoting Teen Involvement in Liturgical Ministry

Because of my role as parish music director, the examples that I use for the following principles for promoting teen involvement in the liturgy are primarily in the area of music ministry. However, the principles can be applied to any liturgical ministry—lectors, eucharistic ministers, greeters—that your parish opens to youth participation. It is my hope that young people are invited into all these ministries.

Strong Parish Leadership That Values Teen Partnership in Ministry

At Saint Blasé it all begins with parish leadership. Our parish leaders—pastor, other clergy, music director, youth ministers, pastoral council, and commission leaders—all understand the value of teen involvement in the parish. The leadership at Saint Blasé truly wants its teens to be involved. They understand the difference between just wanting teens involved in principle, and being willing to do what is necessary to get them involved.

One of the things we found out was that we need to approach teens individually, one on one. Instead of recruiting through the church bulletin, Amy, the director of TLC music ministry, and I directly approach the teens of our parish who we know are musically talented and tell them the parish needs them to sing in the TLC ministry. Our pastoral leaders are alerted to the teens we approach, and they follow up with words of encouragement to these same teens. In essence we've all become genuine salespeople for the TLC ministry.

Our parish leaders deeply desire teen involvement. We are willing to take the first step by approaching teens individually, with a sincere attitude and a true need. We also have a vision for teen involvement—a road map or plan of action that when implemented secures teen participation in our parish.

A Vision for Teen Participation

When Amy broached the idea of creating a teen music ministry at Saint Blasé, she knew what the benefits could be. Amy herself had become involved in music ministry when she was ten years old. I began playing guitar at Saint Blasé liturgies when I was just fifteen years old. Because many of us had been involved in music ministry as teens, a solid vision for youth involvement in music ministry was easily created.

Our vision involved forming a music group of just young people to perform occasionally at the Sunday liturgies. We wanted both a choir and instrumentalists. We intended to start with young people who already had experience singing and playing through school programs and private instruction. And we wanted to use the group primarily as a way of preparing these young people to move on to other roles in our adult music ministries.

But God has a way of expanding your visions. Even though the TLC ministry was initially discussed as a way of bolstering the numbers within our adult music program, TLC became a ministry in its own right. The young people discovered that they had a mission, which built excitement and gave them a reason to want to come together. It also provided a means for identifying those exceptionally talented teens that could, for example, lead our community in song as soloists. And it gave us an avenue for involving youth who never would have been recognized in other areas of parish ministry. And here is the clincher: we had the teens invite other teens that they knew would be interested in joining this ministry. Suddenly a terrific connection was made with a large number of teens in the parish—a connection that ultimately they themselves provided.

When the teens became involved in the TLC ministry, another great connection developed. TLC included several young people who were involved with the youth ministry group in the parish. Relationships between the teens in the music ministry and teens in the youth group began growing, and more of the teens made stronger commitments to the youth program. Admittedly this was not a part of the vision for youth involvement.

But because the initial vision was well developed, many terrific, unforeseen rewards resulted.

The TLC ministry was formed one year after Zack became a part of the contemporary music ministry. Did his involvement have any effect on those twenty teens that initially joined TLC? The answer to that question is in the next section.

Visible Teenage Role Models

I firmly believe that Zack provided a wonderful role model for the teens of Saint Blasé. They had experienced his presence for about a year when the TLC ministry was formed. Coming from another community, Zack was virtually unknown to our parish, but within a few months many of our parishioners knew of this young, talented violin player. All the talk about Zack in our community was positive. When the word went out about creating a new teen music ministry, all the teens had a chance to "be like Zack." Zack paved the way for these teens, and they responded well. How blessed we are that this young man stepped into our community and continues to be a model for all our teens.

We now have many other youth role models. The young people who are currently part of the TLC ministry and those who have moved on from TLC to become part of other groups inspire new youth to participate. Because they prepare well, their ministry is successful—and everyone wants to be part of something successful. With all these young people involved, it is now considered cool to be part of the liturgical ministry at Saint Blasé.

Adult Role Models

Recently I received a visit from a past guitar student who had just completed his second year of college. While studying guitar Tom was very gifted, winning a number of awards in various competitions. He was accepted into the theory program in the school of music at the University of Michigan, where only four students are accepted each year in that specific area of study. Tom's recent visit was for a reason. Though he has been studying math, engineering, and music over the last two years at the U of M, he informed me that he would love to do what I do—become the music director of a parish. Of all the career choices available to this gifted young man, he wanted to pursue church work.

Although I have been the director of music at Saint Blasé for five years, I have been involved in the same contemporary music ministry for twenty-five years. An entire generation of children has watched me minister with a guitar. I am not alone as a long-standing member of the Saint Blasé music program—at least six other people have ministered musically for more than twenty years, and another ten have been ministering for ten years. Children of our community have had many people modeling strong commitment and good ministry for a long time. We have actually begun to see a second generation of music ministers stepping into leadership roles, children of some of those long-standing members becoming cantors and instrumentalists.

The value of role models and the effect they have on teen involvement has been invaluable. Visible mentors have certainly helped pave the way for active teens. But unless our community had truly accepted and appreciated teenage involvement in liturgical ministries, we never could have made the strides we have.

Community Acceptance

A unique set of circumstances has surrounded the music program at Saint Blasé. Until I was hired as director of music, our parish never had an overall director of music. Thus the "folk group" was allowed to operate autonomously. Pastors came and went, and still we were allowed to function independent of an outside leader. Although we made a number of mistakes in our ministering, we were initially seen as a young (90 percent of us were teenagers) and vibrant group. Fortunately the best part of our ministry was the music we made—we were very strong musically; the group was loaded with gifted instrumentalists and singers. In essence we "grew up" in our ministry, in the watchful sight of our community. This experience demonstrated to our entire community that teens were capable of being responsible as well as providing good ministry.

Our community as a whole has continued with this same mind-set. Teens are given a chance and are greatly supported by our community. Sure there are a few people who don't particularly like teen involvement, but they represent a small minority. I thank God that while we were growing up and making the mistakes that all young people make, our community kept supporting us.

To demonstrate our community's acceptance of teen involvement in the parish, let me share one last story. Last year the Voices in Praise choir, our traditional adult choir, held a pancake breakfast as a fund-raiser. When a vote was taken to determine what to do with the money raised, the VIPs unanimously chose to give the majority of it to help pay Zack's way to the Interlochen Summer Music Camp. All the members of the choir saw the value of supporting a teen in his musical development. Needless to say Zack and his family were overwhelmed at this support and generosity.

Unless a parish community gives its full support to teen participation in liturgical ministries, widespread teen involvement will be difficult to achieve. Is the community's support and the circumstances surrounding the participation of teens at Saint Blasé a fluke, or is it possible for others to recreate our success? I believe other churches can experience similar success. I have identified the following strategies from our experience to help pave the way for teen involvement in other parishes. Although there is no perfect formula that can guarantee strong teen participation, I believe that following these suggestions will make a huge difference in developing effective teen involvement in your liturgical ministries.

Strategies for Involving Teens in Liturgical Ministries

1. If the leadership of the parish is the least bit ambivalent about engaging teens in liturgical ministries, the parish will fail in its attempt. The commitment begins with the pastoral team, especially the pastor. The pastor must clearly believe in teen involvement and must demand it from other ministry leaders. Parish leaders must articulate their commitment to teen involvement to the parish as an important first step.
2. A well-thought-out plan of action is critical when considering teen partnership. The vision for teen involvement must be clear and achievable. It must also be shared and agreed upon by all those involved.
3. A teen will commit to an action when approached one-on-one. If it is left up to them to register, sign up, make a phone call, or contact someone, they will likely fail to commit. But present an invitation in person to a teen, and quite often they will readily respond. Make invitations and requests face to face when desiring teen involvement.
4. Invitations must be genuine, and the need for involvement must be real. Teens detect insincerity far better than adults do. And don't think that you can fool a teen into action by giving them meaningless roles or responsibilities. Teens, like all human beings, don't want to waste their time doing trivial things. Make sure you are asking them to do something meaningful, convey the invitation sincerely, and let them know that they are truly needed.

5. Adults must go the "extra mile" to successfully include teenagers. It may take several inquiries with individual teens before they commit, but be patient and keep inviting them. Some teens may say that they are interested and then not show up when needed. Don't immediately write them off. Many adults fail to cut teens any slack in the area of commitment, while they accept miles of excuses from other adults. Even if the commitment is lacking in the beginning, give them the benefit of the doubt. Find out what may have caused the commitment breakdown and see if there is a creative way to respond to it. The more the teen believes in the cause and feels wanted, the more responsible she or he will be—at times even exceeding the commitment of adults.
6. Bend the rules for teens. For example, maybe a teen would like to join the greeter ministry but can't make the quarterly meetings because they fall on Thursday evenings. If they are willing to meet at a different time and can become totally prepared for the responsibilities of the ministry, excuse them from the quarterly meetings. Flexibility is a must when working with teens. Accept that teenagers' schedules are outrageous. Don't let a busy schedule keep a teenager from becoming involved.
7. Negative attitudes will dissuade teens from volunteering. Teens will not work with grumpy, unpleasant people, regardless of the importance of the task. An invitation from an unfriendly, complaining person will not attract a teenager. Successful recruiters of teens are positive people who can show respect and confidence in a teenager's ability to minister. Adults who cannot convey confidence or treat teens with respect will struggle with recruitment.
8. Few teens will become involved with any activity that is not enjoyable. Serious work can also be fun. Good ministry can be pleasant and refreshing. This is important to a teen. Allow for some good-natured joking around in practices. Plan an occasional party after a practice or at the end of a busy liturgical season.
9. If teenagers are going to successfully find their place in a parish community, they cannot be separated from the community at large. When a teen finds church meaningful only when removed from the larger community, the effects can actually be negative. When teens become young adults, they are told they don't belong in a teen setting any longer. Yet because they have been separated from the rest of the

community through their teenage years, they feel completely foreign in the larger community. Make sure your efforts tie teens into your overall program of liturgical ministry.
10. Once teen participation begins, let the active teens become recruiters of new teens. Challenge the active ones to each bring one new teen into their ministry. Visual, active teens will attract other teens. Take advantage of their connections with one another.
11. Publicly praise the active teens. Write articles in the weekend bulletins about their accomplishments. Give them positive feedback and encouragement. Teens struggle (as do most adults) with self-image. Giving them public praise for their commitment and achievements will help them feel good about themselves. This will positively affect their willingness to commit to ministry.
12. Work toward establishing a strong children's choir. This is the breeding ground for future musicians and singers. Maintaining a strong children's choir will build the connection for involvement in ministry as the children grow older.

Active Teens in Liturgical Ministries—It Can Work

Just this past week we have added another talented sixteen-year-old female vocalist to the music program, confirmed plans to sponsor three other teens to attend a weeklong music camp in Minneapolis this summer, and invited two seventh-grade boys to join the TLC ministry. Although the two boys are unsure about singing in the ministry, they said they would give it some thought. The involvement of teenagers within the music program at Saint Blasé is on the rise. Our goal is to involve every teen who is musically gifted and capable of ministering. Lofty as the goal is, we will not rest until we achieve it.

Every talented teen deserves the opportunity to share her or his gifts with the community. We have realized the great rewards that teenagers in ministry offer, and as a result, our worship at Saint Blasé is richer. Teens truly can be a part of good ministry, becoming part of the fabric of the entire community. It is only when adults encourage teens to participate in meaningful liturgical ministries that the wonderful benefits will be realized.

Spirited Music and Singing

Thomas N. Tomaszek

Tom Tomaszek is an author, speaker, composer, and liturgical musician who lives in Milwaukee, Wisconsin. Tom served as project consultant and lead writer for *From Age to Age: The Challenge of Worship with Adolescents* and has contributed to a variety of other youth ministry and liturgical publications, recordings, and resources.

> Let the word of Christ dwell in you richly; teach and admonish one another in all wisdom; and with gratitude in your hearts sing psalms, hymns, and spiritual songs to God. (Col. 3:16)

Music is a significant dimension of how all teens become involved in liturgy. Music is integral to their relationships, including their relationship with God. Music animates their studies, their social time, and their prayer lives. Music speaks their values and shapes their attitudes about what is important in life. Contrary to the stereotype, many youth *want* to sing at Mass. When we truly invite and enable them to take part, teens will raise the roof in song. Youth ministers regularly experience the incredible musical energy of Catholic teens at retreat and conference liturgies, such as the National Catholic Youth Conference or diocesan youth rallies.

The Second Vatican Council wrote about the dynamic between faith, culture, and sacred music in *The Constitution on the Sacred Liturgy* (*Sacrosanctum Concilium,* 1963). The councilors reminded us that first and foremost, the liturgy is the saving work of Christ. Music enables the full, conscious, and active participation of the faithful at the liturgy.

> **The treasure of sacred music is to be preserved and fostered with great care. Choirs must be diligently developed, especially in cathedral churches; but bishops and other pastors of souls must be at pains to ensure that whenever a liturgical service is to be celebrated with song, the whole assembly of the faithful is enabled . . . to contribute the active participation that rightly belongs to it. (No. 114)**

The Constitution on the Sacred Liturgy still serves as our reference point for many liturgical music issues in our own day and age. Subsequent documents such as *Musicam Sacram, Music in Catholic Worship,* and *Liturgical Music Today* addressed many practical and pastoral issues that the Second Vatican Council's renewal began but could not anticipate. However, times have changed, and we now face a variety of new issues that must be addressed.

In *From Age to Age,* youth leaders, liturgists, pastors, parents, and musicians raised four major issues related to music and liturgy under the principle "Vibrant worship has a youthful spirit in music and song." I summarize the issues as (1) balancing musical tradition and renewal, (2) exploring current musical styles for worship, (3) enabling the assembly's musical participation, and (4) using the gifts and talents of young musicians and singers (*From Age to Age,* nos. 64–67).

Balancing Musical Tradition and Renewal

How can we preserve the treasury of sacred music and still be open to the Holy Spirit animating new musical expressions of faith? Sacred music is a vital part of our worship. It needs to be an authentic and living expression of our full, conscious, and active participation at liturgy that carries through to our daily lives. Youth, and other members of the faithful for that matter, want to sing what feels authentically prayerful. They sing when the music and the moment inspire them, as we witness at concerts or other popular cultural events. Teens respond to music, old and new, that captures their heart or feet. In the same way, when liturgical music gives voice to their spirituality, teens sing authentically and enthusiastically.

It is a challenge, however, to find and promote music that enables the participation of *all* members of the liturgical assembly. Our communities are so diverse not only in ages but also in cultures and backgrounds. Yet if we are open to the Holy Spirit working in our midst, we may experience that diversity as a gift and not as an obstacle. *Music in Catholic Worship* noted the challenge that all members of the assembly share:

> **The planning team must consider the general makeup of the total community. Each Christian must keep in mind that to live and worship in community often demands a personal sacrifice. All must be willing to share likes and dislikes with others whose ideas and experiences may be quite unlike their own. (No. 17)**

One of the basic strategies that emerged during the writing of *From Age to Age* was the importance of starting the conversation among local church leaders and young people. A balanced pastoral plan includes the needs of all ages and cultures, which is difficult to achieve. And when it comes to music, we all have an opinion based on our personal preferences and comfort with certain styles and uses. Young people are especially likely to use music to define their identity in certain friendship groups. That doesn't make them musically close-minded, in fact usually it is just the opposite. At parties, school functions, sport practices, and even riding in the car with friends, teens take turns playing their favorite music so that everyone feels included.

Youth are not asking for all liturgical music to be "theirs," however they would like the songs they like to be equally considered as part of the growing tradition. At the 1995 National Youth and Worship Forum they said, "We are not changing tradition, only enhancing it" (*From Age to Age,* p. 5).

When we truly listen to teens without being defensive, we find that they hunger for spiritual connections in their lives. Music helps them express those desires. Music at liturgy can be a powerful, evangelizing witness to the presence of God in their midst.

Strategy 1: Establish a Liturgical Music Advisory Board

A liturgical music advisory board—whether separate from or part of a parish liturgy committee (or commission)—provides the music, choir, or liturgy director with direct feedback on the music selections used at Mass. It is important that such a board represent as much as possible the diverse ages and cultures in the parish community. Too often a parish's liturgical music repertoire is limited to the musical taste of one person. In theory at least, a variety of persons from various life situations should lend their perspective to the music selection process.

The liturgical music advisory board should be advisory and not task specific. That is, the actual selection of music for specific liturgies remains the responsibility of the music director. Artistic, liturgical, and performance factors are involved in choosing music that cannot be decided efficiently by committee vote. To form an effective board, consider the following suggestions:

- Invite a variety of parishioners to become members of the board. Some members of the choir or musical ensembles are necessary, but the best feedback will come from ordinary members of the assembly. Invite some people with admittedly limited voices or those *least* likely to sing, in order to represent that part of the assembly.
- Invite youth to become members of the music advisory board. Invite teens who are involved in bands, choirs, and ensembles at their high school. Keep in mind that some of the best musicians must be "discovered." They may still be too shy to imagine they have a gift to give.
- Invite youth in pairs. Youth are much more willing to volunteer for something when they know a friend is going to be there.
- Make the length of term realistic for youth with school, work, and family commitments. Finding new music and listening to traditional favorites should be part of the learning process for these young people. Many youth spend hours a day listening

to music through their headphones. These teens will be your most conscientious committee members.
- Set monthly or seasonal meetings. The agenda should include a review of music used in the previous season and a preview of options for the coming season. Perhaps here is where key members of the choirs can demonstrate songs, and so on.

Other issues and strategies discussed later in this article may also be agenda items for the liturgical music advisory board.

Strategy 2: Learn to Recognize Youth-Friendly Songs

Learning how to recognize a youth-friendly song when they hear it is one task the liturgical music advisory board members will face. Of course the best way to find these songs is to ask young people themselves. Dick Clark has made a career doing this. Parishes and pastoral ministers can surprise and delight teens, though, by finding songs that are appealing to teen ears. What are the qualities of youth-friendly songs? Let's identify some of these qualities using a particular youth favorite, Michael Joncas's "On Eagles' Wings" as an example.

Beat. The biggest difference between most liturgical music and the music young people listen to daily is the beat. Syncopated or straight, beat is the heart of various music styles from reggae, rock, and rap to hip-hop, alternative, and country. Percussion can help any song become more recognizable and familiar. Even light percussion can help us hear the syncopated pattern in a melody. Beat isn't always obvious, though. The beat in "On Eagles' Wings" comes subtly but surely in the chord progressions: . . . bum, bum, bum . . . "and HOLD you in the palm, 2.3—of His hands." There's movement in that progression that helps the ear along.

Emotive sound. Every song has an identifiable emotive sound that connects with the state of our mind and heart. Obviously our individual response to any song is subjective, but songs have external emotive qualities that can be heard. Youth often use the term upbeat to describe the emotive quality they like in a song. My sense is that "upbeat" means positive feeling, whether the song is fast or slow. "On Eagles' Wings" is a psalm (91) for funerals, which, by its nature, is not an upbeat occasion. Yet our emotive response to the song is positive, a quality of its lyrics and lyrical melody that reminds us that we are held in God's hands.

Intuitively singable. Even though the melody of "On Eagles' Wings" begins high and cascades down through a range any professional singer would love to own, ordinary voices are still able to sing it. The note progressions are intuitive and predictable, even when they jump a third or fourth. Untrained voices in the assembly, particularly young people not accustomed to singing in groups, find that quality of a song comforting.

Melodic hook. Popular songs also have memorable melodies that capture our attention even without lyrics. They have a "hook," or progression of notes, that stays in our creative brain and often rattles around for days. Melodic hook is perhaps the most subjective quality of a song. We can recognize it even in songs we don't like. "On Eagles' Wings" certainly possesses a melodic hook that has been played on a variety of instruments and has been hummed by many a person on their way out of church.

Rhythm. Who could ask for anything more? Well, beyond beat, every song has a rhythm that is a product of its time signature, pace, and length of notes. Several observable factors help make songs "cool." Most popular music is written in 4/4, or common time. The four beats in each measure seem to give the composer more freedom with note intervals. On the other hand, much of our liturgical music repertoire is in 3/4 time. Three beats in each measure seem to match up more easily with the liturgical texts and psalms. (At least that's my theory.) Songs in 3/4 can be "cool," but they have to work harder for the attention of ears that hear quite a bit of music in 4/4 time. Many wonderful and prayerful songs are set in 3/4 time as well as nonrhythmic modes such as chant. But I don't think it is a coincidence that the ever popular "On Eagles' Wings" is written in 4/4.

Text. Liturgical and ritual music becomes our prayer as a community. Our united voices become a symbol that we are the Body of Christ gathered in his name, responding to his invitation "to do this in memory of me." Therefore, if the song texts used at liturgy don't help us pray that group identity, they fall short of their purpose. This is a major difference between music created specifically for liturgy and songs that we hear on the radio. It is very hard for most young people to understand this distinction. As often-used as "On Eagles' Wings" is, the lyrics give expression to our communal identity with its beautiful and powerful imagery: the breath of dawn, terrors of the night, being held in the palm of God's hands. These are words that connect at a deep, emotional level for the singer and listener. Ask young people to identify other liturgical songs that speak to their heart. You will be surprised they were listening.

Exploring Current Musical Styles for Worship

We can balance the pastoral plan for all ages and cultures by using a variety of musical styles. The Second Vatican Council suggested that "the people's own religious songs are to be encouraged with care so that in sacred devotions as well as during services of the liturgy itself, in keeping with rubrical norms and requirements, the faithful may raise their voices in song" (*Constitution on the Sacred Liturgy,* no. 118).

The councilors were concerned that liturgical renewal lead all the faithful to a "full, conscious and active participation" (*Constitution on the Sacred Liturgy,* no. 14). They believed that music was integral to increasing that participation from various cultural groups. Music is also essential to increasing the participation of young people in our own culture. How will their religious songs become part of the musical treasury we use at worship?

Many of today's Catholic teens have learned a repertoire of religious songs at youth rallies and national events, and from their Christian friends. These contemporary spiritual songs and the artists who sing them reflect the diversity of popular musical styles. In fact, Christian music *is* a current musical genre that has increased in popularity, especially in the last ten to fifteen years. Because these songs have a spiritual quality to them and are often based on the Scriptures, Catholic teens wonder if we can use them for parish liturgies. How should we respond? If a contemporary spiritual song fulfills the pastoral, musical, and liturgical judgments, why *not* use it? (See *Music in Catholic Worship,* nos. 26–41). My sense is that musical *style,* not musical *quality* more often influences our parish selections.

Sacred music by its nature embraces a variety of traditional and contemporary styles. Immediately after Vatican Council II, the musical styles of the popular culture of the late 1960s and early 1970s strongly influenced the music that we used at our "renewed" liturgies. Pianos and guitars shifted our musical focus from choirs to instrumental ensembles. The people responded actively, perhaps because the songs seemed closer to their daily spiritual lives but also because the folk music styles of the protest movement encouraged and required participation. In that way they were a great fit for liturgy with a renewed sense of the role of the faithful gathered. Thankfully our liturgical repertoire continued to develop more complex melodies and scripturally based texts. In some ways, however, as the music and musicianship have matured, we have lost that same sense of necessary participation. Too many people in the assembly are content to watch and listen.

The musical styles of the post–Vatican II generation continue to influence much of our current liturgical music repertoire. Today a new generation of young people asks why its popular music styles are not considered worthy for worship. Can amplified and synthesized sounds, percussion, and syncopated rhythms also be used to give God praise? Is there room in our definitions of sacred music for percussive beats? Is a tenor sax solo any less prayerful than a flute?

Sacred music by its nature also needs to be culturally inclusive. Does our current understanding of sacred music include that of African, Caribbean, South and Central American, Mexican, Asian, Pacific, and other cultures in addition to those of Europe? The diversity of our society requires that we foster the fullness of our sacred musical heritage. All members of the assembly need to have a respect for the music of others. We all need to grow in our appreciation of the diversity with which God has blessed us.

Music in Catholic Worship states the need to examine musical styles so that all the faithful can pray: "The music used [at liturgy] should be within the competence of most of the worshipers. It should suit their age-level, cultural background, and level of faith" (no. 15). For young people beat and pace are key musical style concerns. It is the *energy* of a song that catches them up in prayer. However, that does not mean that youth like only songs that are fast and loud. They have many favorite reflective and slower paced songs. Teens also appreciate choral music. Many are involved in choirs and classical ensembles in their local high schools. They appreciate melodies and poetic texts that touch their heart, soul, and rhythm of life. Most of all, youth appreciate music played or sung with enthusiasm. Young people find it easier to add their voice when the whole assembly sings strongly.

Strategy 3: Expand and Develop the Parish Music Repertoire

Every parish has a repertoire of familiar music that is used regularly for Sunday Masses. That list and its rotation need to include selections that are particularly appealing to teens and people of diverse cultures. At a workshop I recently facilitated, one young person said to the adult participants: "You have to give something to get something. If you want more youth participation, you need to give something in return." One way to respond to this young man's challenge is to use songs that teens request. Young people would love to help! Here are a few steps toward expanding the parish music repertoire.

Survey youth. We may be surprised by which songs comprise young people's church music Top 40. Survey youth at a regularly scheduled youth ministry gathering or religious education event. Take along hymnals or a sampling of the worship aids and have youth choose their favorite songs. You can also invite a small focus group of youth to provide input and ideas.

Change the arrangements. You can also expand the repertoire by adding different instrumentation or a fresh arrangement to a familiar song. For example, add an instrumental solo to begin the piece or as an interlude; add a new harmony or descant line; change the tempo or time signature; change the key; change the instrumentation by adding synthesizer, guitar, piano, or percussion; or change the vocal leads on certain verses.

Know your assembly's likes and dislikes. Although liturgy is not performance, it always has a performance dimension for liturgical musicians. Some assemblies respond better when there is a strong cantor or song leader. Other congregations grow quiet. Some parishes learn new music quickly and are bored just as quickly. Other groups need months to learn one new set of acclamations.

Listen to new music together. Several parishes who have begun to implement the strategies in *From Age to Age* asked leaders from the various parish choirs and ensembles to meet together to listen to new music. Together they choose a half dozen new songs that all groups will commonly learn and use in the next liturgical season.

Visit other parishes. Research is always helpful. Sometimes the best research may be down the street, across the city, or in a neighboring denomination. Have members of your choir or ensemble take a field trip in lieu of one week's practice time. Creative sparks will ignite new energy for familiar material.

Create a music rotation list. Do you keep a record of which songs are used each year? Sometimes it may help to take certain songs out of rotation for a period of time. You can breathe new life into these selections by *not* using them. When they return, these songs will feel more like a comfortable old shoe that is easy to step into. Ever wonder why "oldies" stations are popular? We might learn from this dynamic in our selection of liturgical music.

Enabling the Assembly's Musical Participation

Prior to the Second Vatican Council, the congregation's role at Mass was more receptive than active. Father said the Mass and we listened, stood, sat, or knelt as we followed the Latin in our missals. The choir sang the songs, although we usually helped to sing the entrance, offertory, communion, or closing hymns. Now it seems we are always singing something—acclamations, intercessions, psalms, antiphons. Many Catholics do not understand that music is normative for liturgy.

Singing gives symbolic expression to our common faith, but many members of the assembly, particularly youth, are still in the listening mode. Some youth are not ready to sing their own song, let alone the song of the church. Others are in a period of questioning their parents' beliefs. A lack of parental example has discouraged others. For those reasons, *all* the ways we reach out to youth—through social, catechetical, and service experiences—will have an impact on their liturgical participation, including their singing. For the moment, however, their participation may simply be their presence on Sundays.

Are there any solutions? Choosing music that is user-friendly is one way to communicate acceptance to these young faith seekers in our midst. Involving teens in the musical ensembles is another. But it is my experience that feeling the desire to sing in church is an "attitude adjustment" that happens in individuals and in groups over a period of time. Even youth-friendly music played by teens will be ignored if the attitude of not singing prevails. Look around on Sundays—the young people who are not singing are often sitting with parents and peers who are not singing. The reverse is also true. At national youth events, everyone sings—loudly. A pervasive attitude of participation allows teens who *never* sing back home to add full voice.

How can we change people's attitudes? First of all we have to change our attitude. This may be difficult for some of us dedicated musicians to hear directly, but if we want the assembly to sing, we have to put more of our energy into supporting their singing and put less attention on our own choirs and ensembles. Obviously we need to do both, and when choirs and ensembles really function as song leaders, they *do* enable the assembly. We need to employ effective techniques and strategies for teaching music and inviting participation instead of demanding it.

The second factor that may need to be adjusted to increase assembly singing is the sound of the accompaniment. Too many of our liturgical ensembles are not loud enough for timid voices. When they built the majestic cathedrals in Europe, the designers installed huge pipe organs that literally rocked the walls with wonderful sounds. (Youth understand this concept. Just listen to the bass in their cars as they drive by on the road.) A single piano, guitar, or less-than-adequate organ is just not a big enough sound to support a large assembly of voices.

Strategy 4: Develop the Liturgical Music Ensembles

We can support assembly singing by strengthening and enlarging the musical ensembles that accompany them. Youth and young adults can be instrumental (pun intended) in creating these diverse accompaniments. Consider some of the following ideas:

Add other instruments. If you use only organ or piano, consider adding guitars and a synthesizer. If you use only a tambourine for percussion, try adding congas, a snare drum, or cymbals. Electric bass is particularly helpful in establishing a solid beat for new arrangements. Woodwinds, saxophone especially, and horns can add variety and spice to existing arrangements.

People notice these changes and feel energized to participate. Many young people already play these instruments and would be honored if invited to share their talents with the community. Ask the local high school music teachers, band and choir directors, and guidance counselors for referrals. These professionals can tell you of teens' musical abilities, and, in the process, you will establish a working relationship that will help you overcome scheduling or practicing conflicts in the future.

Seek out musical arrangers. Adding instruments creates a nightmare for an overworked or underqualified music leader. Many young adults who are pursuing music careers would be delighted to have projects for which to use their music notation software. Identify four or five new pieces for each liturgical season that could use arranging, and then ask these talented young people to supply arrangements for the particular set of instruments that are available.

Go slowly. Your efforts will be far more successful if you keep a long-range plan in mind. Build your ensembles piece by piece, step by step so that the assembly isn't overwhelmed and you have the ability to do each step well. Adding a synthesizer or percussion that is poorly played will do more to turn off those who are skeptical than to turn on those who are receptive.

Strategy 5: Review and Update the Sound System

One of the biggest stumbling blocks to effective ensembles is the lack of an adequate sound system. Parishes need a system with the ability to amplify other instruments and voices, and sufficient for the size of the worship space. The cost of equipment is reasonable in proportion to the achievement of your goal of full participation.

Youth and adults who are already employed in music or electronics industries would be honored and enthused to help evaluate, price, or set up amplification for instruments and voices. Teens would love to hold a fund-raiser in support of sound equipment. Use their gifts wisely!

Using the Gifts and Talents of Young Musicians and Singers

Young people can play a special role in choosing and creating liturgical music that celebrates diversity. We need to find specific ways to invite and enable their musical gifts. The participants at the 1995 National Youth and Worship Forum stated, "Youth want to become involved in the choir/music of the liturgy" (*From Age to Age*, p. 15). Many teens have been taking music lessons since they were small children. Many youth and young adults are already skilled in musical technologies that can enhance our parish worship.

Will we allow young people to give their musical gifts without expecting them to make impossible adult commitments? We put so much effort and time into developing children's choirs and then stop offering an opportunity for participation when these young people reach high school (see *The Directory for Masses with Children,* no. 30). The reason is usually difficulty in accommodating teens' busy schedules. Maybe we need to rethink their commitment from a weekly to a seasonal or annual contribution. For example, allowing a young keyboard player to help only during Lent and Easter might enable her to be involved in fall sports or a group of madrigal singers. Youth are trying out many different roles and activities. They should not have to make adult-level commitments to be involved.

Jesus' most public miracle was feeding the multitudes with the simple gifts of a young person (John 6:1–14). Christ will continue to miraculously feed our communities if we are also willing to call forth the simple gifts of today's adolescents. At the 1995 National Youth and Worship Forum, which provided input for *From Age to Age,* many teens sadly said they were not allowed to participate in parish liturgy preparation. How can young people understand and value our tradition if we always keep them isolated from our planning and decision-making processes? Likewise how can we pay attention to the Holy Spirit's movement in the church and in the world, as the Second Vatican Council reminded us, without the eyes and ears of youth? (*Constitution on the Sacred Liturgy,* no. 43).

Strategy 6:
Apprentice Youth in Liturgy Preparation and Music Selection

In many ways we are rediscovering the importance of apprenticing or mentoring our young people into adult roles and responsibilities. What many other cultures take for granted, we have lost in our segmented and specialized society. If we wish to truly develop the musical and liturgical gifts of this generation, we must be intentional in our support and guidance. As a by-product, adult mentors often have their own love for their ministry reawakened by their involvement with the young people.

I suggest you start by having youth apprentice key liturgical leaders, including the pastoral musician, the sacristan, the ministries coordinator, the head of hospitality or ushers, and the art and environment coordinator. These adult ministers should meet with the youth apprentices to show them how they prepare for and carry out their ministry. In appropriate ways the young people can be invited to share in the ministry, discovering and developing their own gifts and skills under the mentor's guidance. I have found the following approaches important in developing a successful liturgical apprenticeship program:

- Be sure the invitation for both the youth and the adults is personal and based on observed talents rather than a general call for volunteers. Expect some initial rejections. Remember that most youth are still trying to believe that they are good at *anything*. Your persistence is important to their self-discovery.
- Take Noah's approach and invite youth two by two. Teens are much more willing to say yes when they know a friend is going to be with them. The visibility of some youth will promote interest in other teens.
- Designate recruiters. Only a few teens will respond to parent urging or will choose to help on their own. Peers can help with recruitment, but the best approach is to identify several recruiters who can get referrals from high school music or choir directors.
- Set the apprenticeships for a fixed length of time, such as six months or one year, but allow them to be renewed if both

parties agree. Youth should not have to make lifelong commitments to these roles. As adolescents they need the freedom to explore the range of their gifts and talents.
- The adult leaders should be open to the plan and not coerced into becoming mentors. Make it clear that they are not giving up their role but sharing responsibilities. Emphasize that the teens are not just assistants but need to experience the difficulty of balancing tradition with current needs. The mentors are helping the parish and church invest in its ongoing renewal and future leadership. In a very direct way, these mentors are encouraging vocations to ministry.
- Use World Youth Day Sunday each year (the thirtieth Sunday of Ordinary Time in the United States) as the marker for announcing the apprenticeships. Commission the mentors and apprentices at the weekend Masses and list their names in the weekly order of worship or parish bulletin. The National Federation of Catholic Youth Ministry creates an annual resource book full of ideas, prayers, activities, and liturgical suggestions for celebrating World Youth Day.
- Send these young apprentices to diocesan leadership events and training days. We make it easier for youth when we offer training as a part of the plan. No one wants to feel uncomfortable or ill prepared to do a task. Youth are quick to learn. They will bring back fresh ideas and insights to the parish. In the process they will increase awareness of current spiritual concerns of the diocese.
- You will need to confront many of the political obstacles of parish life. Let your efforts be a visible witness of the parish's commitment to youth and an encouragement to other teens to use their gifts and talents in God's service.

Conclusion

Finally, keep all these elements in their proper perspective. Life in Christ is our mission. Music gives voice to our praise as faithful members of the Body of Christ. As we celebrate the sacred mysteries with young people, we give God thanks for their vitality and charisms. Their voices, added to ours, sing the glory of God, from age to age.

Ten Things to Keep in Mind When Preaching to Youth

Bishop Kenneth Untener

Bishop Untener is the ordinary of the Diocese of Saginaw, Michigan. He is a popular conference speaker and the author of several books on liturgy. His latest book, *Is Preaching Better? Practical Suggestions for Homilists,* is published by Paulist Press.

Before giving some specifics about preaching to youth, I want to say a word about the pre-homily mind-set of the homilist—some thoughts about what ought to be running through our brain during the preparation of this kind of homily and during those moments when we're stepping up to do it. Don't think about a "crowd of youth." Think about a couple of your nieces and nephews. Picture specific, real people whom you know well and who know you and respect you.

You would be surprised by what a difference this makes. It is not unlike the best tip I ever got on how to handle a television interview. When I was a young priest and had to go before the TV cameras for the first time, a crusty old public relations fellow took me aside and said something like this: "Now look. I don't want you to go out there and think you are talking to one hundred thousand people at a football stadium. What you're actually doing is talking to a couple of people in their living room at home. Think about them and what you'd like to say to them, and then go out there and *talk to them.*"

A crowd of young people can seem a formidable group, just like the group we (mistakenly) picture when going before TV cameras. If that is our mind-set when writing a homily for youth, we will write the wrong kind of homily, and we will try to "perform" when we go out there to give it. But if instead we write something we would say to a couple of our nieces and nephews, and speak as we would to them, it comes from the heart, and the young people out there quickly sense that we are talking to each of them, not performing for a crowd. It makes all the difference in the world.

With that as a backdrop, I'll set forth the best tips I've learned from thirty-five years of preaching to young people. They're especially important in a homily at a youth gathering, but they also apply to any homily where youth are present in the assembly, which of course is most homilies.

1. It Is a Homily

The most important thing to keep in mind is that a homily to young people is still a homily. Homiletics is the ministry of discerning what the Lord is doing and speaking through this event, and helping to engage the people in this. The key is what the *Lord* is doing. The *event* is the convergence of

- these Scripture texts
- this liturgical setting
- this time and place
- these people

In this case "these people" are young people. We take that into account as we would if "these people" were a gathering of senior citizens, or religious, or attorneys at a red Mass. In all cases, however, it is still a homily. This simple truth is most forgotten at special events.

Our sole purpose is to help these young people open themselves to the flow of God's grace in this liturgy. It is most of all God's grace that is at work here, not our skill or cleverness.

Of course the vocabulary, the examples, the stories will be tailored to the group. But in crafting these, we are subject to the subtle temptation of thinking that our artfulness is the primary *cause* of the good results of this event. Not so. It is the Lord. In our homily, unless we minister what the Lord is doing, we are off the track.

Once we realize this, it is actually a relief. We may not be greatly skilled at entertaining young people, but we have a good shot at helping along what the Lord is doing in the liturgical event. Focus on that.

2. The Homily Is Not the Main Event

On certain occasions we unconsciously have the impression that our homily is the most important part of the liturgy. This happens easily at major funerals, at Christmas and Easter, at parish centennials, and at Masses for young people. We forget that besides the homily there is the ritual, and most of the event is the ritual, and the ritual is the most important part of the event.

When you think about it, symbols are more likely to speak to young people than anything else, and our liturgical symbols are sacred and grace filled. Those who plan the liturgy (and the homilist is usually part of this) should see to it that the young people in attendance are given every opportunity for full, conscious, active participation in the fundamental actions of the liturgy. Once again, it is God who is at work, and we are simply ministers to help along what God is doing.

In preparing to preach to young people, we need to step back and put the homily in the larger perspective.

3. Don't Moralize

Homilists have been taught to be practical, down to earth, to connect with real life. As a result the pattern of many homilies is this: *(a)* we say something about the Scriptures of the day; *(b)* we use this as a basis for some do's and don'ts. (The latter is what I mean by "moralizing.")

For example, let's say we have the Gospel in which Jesus says, "You are the salt of the earth . . . you are the light of the world" (Matt. 5:13–14). We follow the usual pattern: *(a)* we explain the images of salt and light and remind the parishioners that this is part of the Sermon on the Mount, which is intended for all disciples; *(b)* we make some applications about how we are supposed to make a difference in our world (salt) and give good example (light).

If we were to use this pattern, our applications (part b) at a youth Mass would all revolve around the real-life circumstances of young people. For example, as "salt" they should get involved in issues at school and not always go along with the things that make them popular with their classmates, and as "light" they should have the courage to let other teenagers know that they have certain moral values and also be good examples to their younger brothers and sisters. The more concrete we are in our application and the more we demonstrate that we know teenagers, the better the homily.

Wrong.

For one thing, they've heard it all before. It's predictable stuff. For another, we don't change people's behavior by telling them what to do. We change behavior by helping them see things differently. And that is what a homily is supposed to do: open our eyes to the great mystery of God proclaimed in the Scriptures, and thus help us to see life differently.

The mistake is to use something in the Scriptures as the *occasion* to say something about real life but without any serious engagement of the text. We use the text as a peg, a thought-starter, and then go on with our own development.

Changed behavior really comes from seeing things differently, which is what a homily is supposed to help us do. We try to help the light of the Scriptures and God's grace open us up to a deeper, wider perspective, a richer understanding of life.

Let's outline another approach using the same Gospel text:

Stop and think for a moment about what we say when we talk to ourselves. The truth is, we tend to put ourselves down: "You dummy!" "What a fool I am."

Interesting. What does Jesus say when he talks to you? "You are the salt of the earth . . . you are the light of the world." In the Gospel he said this to regular folks—not the big hitters, the highly educated religious leaders in Jerusalem, but to the people up north in Galilee . . . the farmers and fishermen and shepherds and small-town people. And he said it "live" to you when this Gospel was proclaimed. He says it "live" to you every minute of every day.

He doesn't say this to you because you have a wonderful family background—maybe you do and maybe you don't. He doesn't say this to you because you're doing so well in school—maybe you are and maybe you aren't. He says this to you because he made you that way.

I've made for you some small cards that simply have those words on them: "You are the salt of the earth. You are the light of the world." Put one someplace in your room—maybe in your sock drawer—somewhere where you'll see it at the beginning of every day. I guarantee you: your day will be different.

No moralizing. No telling them what to do or what not to do. No one leaves with an extra burden. We simply go to the heart of the mystery of creation and the mystery of God's love for us. They'll see God, life, and themselves a bit differently. And *that* is what affects behavior.

4. Be Relatively Brief

It is my theory that at special events we should follow this principle: the bigger the event, the shorter the homily. Again, the homily is not the centerpiece of the Mass.

At special events we have the illusion that the homily should be special, and we translate "special" to mean "longer." The truth is, such events don't require a major-size homily. And contrary to our preconceptions, people will not be disappointed if the homily is relatively brief. It's hard to convince ourselves of this.

In preparing a homily for such gatherings, we should picture the homily as small. Instead of presenting a string of sensational thoughts, all we need to do is give them a pearl to take home with them. If we think this way during our preparation, we're more apt to look for a gem that we can carefully polish and put into a setting. It's liberating to approach it this way. All we have to do is discern a core thought that will help the flow of God's grace and then go to the depth of it. A good thought has plenty of richness and unfolds into a full-fledged homily.

At special events we don't have to be more clever, to come up with an array of terrific thoughts. All we need is a pearl with depth, which leads into the next thought.

5. Young People Deserve Depth

Young people are used to adults who try to demonstrate that they are tuned in to teenage thinking (which, though at times deep, has its share of shallowness). They catch it right away and squirm at the scenario of a forty-year-old trying to do this.

How do we reach young people? With depth. The deeper we go, the more we connect with anyone of any age.

Preach the great mysteries of God. These are the truths that produce wonder and awe and that change people's lives. Most preaching neglects these. We assume the great truths and move quickly into moralizing.

When we focus on the underlying essentials of our faith, our homilies may not seem as sensational, innovative, or clever. But the effects will be formative, with long-range and far-reaching effects. I have two criteria for a great homily: (1) the parishioners remember it; (2) the memory helps them. Both elements are important. We can accomplish the first by saying something that is bizarre, tricky, neat, or funny. But the memory of it doesn't necessarily help people live their lives.

Young people recognize and appreciate depth. (They also recognize shallowness.)

6. Stay with One Thought

Based on my informal and ongoing survey of Catholics these past twenty-five years, the most frequent criticism of homilies is this: "too many thoughts." (I was surprised, thinking that *numero uno* would be "too long.")

Trying to touch on too many thoughts is a particular danger of homilies directed to young people. There are a lot of things we need to tell them, so we try to tell them a lot of things.

There is another reason. It is easier to skim along the surface of several thoughts than to take one and go deep. I believe this to be *the* reason why so many homilies don't stay with one thought.

In my fifth principle I mentioned that young people deserve depth. The way to force ourselves to go deep is to say to ourselves: I'm going to stay with one thought, and I'm going to take it to its depths. People respond to depth, and this includes young people.

7. Get Right into It

Particularly at "special" Masses, the introductory off-the-cuff stuff in homilies tends to go on a bit. We talk about how we felt when we were asked to preach . . . or about some things that happened while we were preparing the homily. . . . We mention some of the people present . . . or what happened just before Mass . . . or anything. We're nervous, we want to connect, or we want to get their attention.

I see three problems with this introductory stuff: (1) we take up precious time, usually more than we think; (2) there is clearly a shift when we finish these openers and get into our message, and it is a signal that "here comes the boring religious stuff"; (3) it is unnecessary because, unlike most other talks, we have their total attention from the start. The last thing we need is an attention getter. Just look around after the Gospel is proclaimed. The people are seated in utter stillness. The trick is to hold their attention, not to get it.

One of the best tips I ever heard about teaching homilists came from one of the folks in the pew who said, "Tell them to go right to the middle of it." This tip is especially important for those who preach to youth. Don't start them off with fluff. Let them know right from the beginning that we take them seriously and are here to say something worthwhile. Go right to the heart of it.

8. If You Use a Story or Example, Make Sure It Is a Helpful One

People love stories. And they remember stories. So when we use a story, we should make sure it carries the thought we want them to remember.

I have observed three different kinds of stories in homilies:

A story or example whose main purpose is to get attention, entertain, loosen people up. We can usually find some way of connecting such stories to the event we are celebrating, but often it's a stretch. These stories don't really throw any light on our "pearl." They're more diversion than enlightenment. Nothing would be missing if the story were left out. Generally speaking, such stories don't belong in homilies . . . but we tend to use them often when speaking to young people. Resist the temptation.

A story or example that illumines the message. These stories serve a purpose. They are like good wine that enhances the taste of a meal. If they were left out, the message would not be as clear or forceful. That is the difference between this kind of story and the kind mentioned in the preceding paragraph. Stories and examples with a purpose enrich any homily.

A story or example that *is* the message. These stories don't simply illustrate the message. They are in themselves the message and don't need further development. The best examples are the parables of Jesus. When he told the story of the prodigal son, there was nothing more to say. All the listeners had to do was think about it, and keep thinking about it, which people have done for centuries.

Writing such stories takes considerable skill. But if the homilist is up to it, these kinds of stories are excellent, especially with young people. Everyone can take it into their own life and make the application without us beating them over the head.

One caveat about stories: many are too long. Telling a story is easy, and we've got the people's full attention. They enjoy the story, and we enjoy telling it. So we take our time and include details unnecessary to the point. (This often happens in conversations when someone is telling a joke.) The parables of Jesus were remarkably concise. We should imitate them.

9. If Possible, Use a Prop or Visual Aid

Props or visual aids can greatly enhance any homily. For various reasons we feel freer to use them with young people. Fine. Use them, if you can use them with integrity.

Props or visual aids should never be simply entertainment or attention getters. Their sole purpose is to illuminate the core thought of the homily. Young people (actually, any people) can tell right away if we're using a prop simply to "hook" them and then, with slight of hand, turn to the religious stuff—like a soup kitchen where, after eating, the people have to listen to the preaching. The test of a good prop is if we can hold it in our hand and occasionally refer to it throughout the entire homily.

A prop has two good results: (1) it gets the attention of the young people (they're all looking at it); (2) it helps the homilist focus on one thought (i.e., the thought illuminated by the prop that we're holding). Another advantage is that we tend to be more natural, creative, and concrete when we're using a prop.

So if at all possible, use a prop or visual aid when preaching to young people. (It might free us to do it more often with adults, which would be a plus.)

10. Speak from the Heart

There's a difference between speaking *at* the young people (or trying to identify with them or act like them, which usually comes across as phony) and simply speaking from the heart. When we speak from the heart, we are ourselves, they are themselves, and they can tell that we love them and care about them. It's genuine, and the medium is a major part of the message.

Here is the best way to do this: Prepare the homily as you usually would. Go over it so that you get hold of the heart of what you want to say. Don't memorize every point, just get the heart of it, and know it so well that you could say it six different ways.

Then let go of everything you prepared and go out there and from the heart speak the core thought you could give six different ways.

Do you know what's difficult about that? We're afraid we'll lose some of the "points" that are part of our development, or some of the clever things we were going to say. So we memorize the whole outline point by point to make sure we include everything. It's like stacking up boxes and then going out there and handing them out one at a time.

It would be far, far better to prepare well and then go out there and speak from the heart without worrying about all those great pieces we'll forget to use.

"Well," you might say, "what if I leave out the core of what I was going to say?" Impossible. Not if what you have to say revolves around one pearl and you've taken it into your own heart.

Just recently I preached at a high school baccalaureate Mass. It was unbearably hot, the crowded church was not air-conditioned, and everyone was all dressed up. It didn't take a genius to know that this was not the time for even a regular-size homily. So I began by saying, "It's hot. So I'm going to pitch most of what I prepared and simply tell you the heart of what I wanted to say." It was as easy as could be. I wasn't worried about looking good, sounding good, or including everything I had prepared. All I wanted to do was give them the core. It came straight from the heart, lasted about five minutes, and was far, far better than what I would otherwise have done. Too bad I needed the heat to make me do it.

There are other things to keep in mind when preaching to young people. Most of all, remember: We don't need gimmicks to preach to young people. Rather we need faithfulness to the ministry of what the Lord is doing in this event and—something we can't put together in a week—holiness.

Training Youth for Liturgical Drama

Sheila O'Connell-Roussell

Sheila O'Connell-Roussell is a campus minister and religion teacher at Saint Mary's Academy in Portland, Oregon. She is a gifted singer, songwriter, and playwright. Sheila has a bachelor's degree in theater arts, a master's in religious education, a master's of divinity, and a doctorate in ministry.

From age to age Christ has gathered a people to himself, a church who would celebrate and proclaim his life, teachings, death, and Resurrection. As did our ancestors in faith, we of this age do this in the context of sacred liturgy. Our liturgy is the work of the whole family of Christ, young and old alike. The art of liturgical drama is a gift that incarnates our skills, talents, and passion for the word of God—helps us create vibrant liturgy by enabling the Word to become flesh through the instrument of the human body. By involving youth in liturgical drama, we offer them a place and purpose in the liturgy of the word, an opportunity to celebrate their baptismal vows, to exercise a ministerial function that "breaks open" the Scriptures in a new way for all of us.

As we enter the birth pangs of the third millennium, we must recognize that our youth are the single most technologically sophisticated, media savvy, visual group to have walked Mother Earth. Visual drama can speak to them more powerfully than the spoken word alone. Thus liturgical drama can be a powerful way for them to enter into the liturgical celebration. I have witnessed many bored young people become excited about their faith through their participation in liturgical drama.

In this article I will first attempt to give a brief history of the place of liturgical drama in the church and name some opportunities available to us today to practice it. Then I will lead you through the steps I take to prepare a group to do liturgical drama. I will not be providing actual drama scripts because there are many drama resources already available. What I find, however, is that many people lack experience in preparing a group of potential performers spiritually. I hope this article will assist you in doing that.

Liturgical Drama in the Church

The spiritual formation of any group of liturgical players is rooted in the church's long tradition known as the sacred mission of the artist. Your troupe of players is connected through the mystical body of Christ with all those holy men and women who passed on the sacred stories of salvation through their artistic gifts offered to God. Here's a quick overview to help you make those connections.

A Brief History of Liturgical Drama

Our Jewish Roots: Sacred Storytellers, Singers, and Dancers

Our Jewish ancestors in faith have long recognized the gifts of artists as sanctified. The inspired writers of the Scriptures were sacred storytellers and performers. Miriam sang of freedom and danced before the Lord, choreographing and directing the women to join her (Exod. 15:20–21). The warrior Judith sang of victory with praises to God (Jth. 14:14). King David is remembered as a poet and a composer of religious music. The Scriptures recall that as David led those who carried the ark of the Covenant, he danced with "all the house of Israel . . . before the Lord with all their might, with songs and lyres and harps and tambourines and castanets and cymbals" (2 Sam 6:4–5). References to the gifts of the musician and the singer fill the Psalms, and the craft of the artist is celebrated as being "filled . . . with divine spirit" (Exod. 31:1–6; 35:35).

Jesus the Storyteller

Embracing the privilege of passing on the tradition of salvation, we also take as our model Jesus the storyteller. As Jesus gathered a community around him, he spun tales that celebrated timeless and universal spiritual and ethical truths woven within symbols understood by the common people of his time. Those who followed our Lord remembered his words and how they changed their lives, and they passed on the stories.

Courage in the Early Church

The birth of Christianity took place in a time of Roman persecution. We find names of early Christian theater artists among the martyrs from those troubled times. Cecilia, patron of music, and Genesius, patron of theater, are two in particular who are role models for those practicing liturgical drama.

Saint Cecilia: patron of music. Saint Cecilia was a Roman youth in the third century who consecrated herself to Christ. She spent her days making musical instruments and writing spiritual music to honor her Lord. As was the law at the time, she was called before the Roman magistrate and ordered to burn a sacrifice of incense before the image of the emperor. Cecilia refused to honor Caesar as divine and was condemned to death, but not before converting her persecutors to Christ with her virtue and courage.

Saint Genesius: patron of the theater. Saint Genesius was a third-century Roman actor, a comedian who performed anti-Christian satire. However, during one performance he had a profound mystical experience. Legend has it that Christ stood before him on the stage and asked a well-known question, "Why do you persecute me?" In one moment Genesius went from mocking Christianity to embracing Jesus as Lord right in front of that Roman audience. He was ordered to deny his testimony. With tenacity and saintly courage, the actor faced death for refusing to deny the reality of his relationship with Christ.

Freedom for the Artist: Liturgical Drama in the Middle Ages

When Emperor Constantine issued the Edict of Toleration, ending three hundred years of bloody persecutions in Rome, Christian artists were free to publicly express their faith through their craft. In the early Christian church, the theater arts were suspect due to their connection to the pagan religious theater cults of the Greco-Roman world. However, by the Middle Ages, drama had come to be seen as a valid and essential ministry in the church. Theater was a civic event supported by church, state, and citizen. Most of this theater celebrated saints and religious events through pageants, religious festivals, and sacred dramas. The cast was made up of members of the community—trade guilds, clerics and laity, all ranks and professions. Theater pageants, processions, and celebrations honoring the feast of Corpus Christi became known virtually in every community in Christendom, making theater the accepted way to observe the sacred stories of the faith.

The challenge we face today in reclaiming the role of sacred drama in the liturgy is that our society denigrates art to the level of decoration and entertainment. The sacred artist has a mission to live in stark contrast to this poverty of perception, to help us rediscover sacred drama as a means of evangelization. The arts possess immeasurable potential for good, if crafted toward sacred purpose.

Sacred Drama: Evangelization for Today

As we enter the third millennium, religious educators, spiritual directors, and pastoral ministers are encountering a type of cultural Christianity that is not familiar with the sacred and formative stories of the Judaic-Christian traditions. Yet the fostering of Catholic identity requires Christians to *re-member* our spiritual foundation, to reinterpret the sacred stories for this age, and to develop a hermeneutic for this generation. Liturgical drama has the power to do this, and in doing so becomes an expression of the liturgy of the word, part of the sacramental remembering.

Memory as Icon of the Presence

Sacramental memory is not a passive recalling, like what might be suggested by the word *remember* in modern English. This remembering is a prophetic recommitment to the mission of Christ. This *memory* embraces a pledge to make one's mind fully attuned, a commitment to *be fully aware* and inflamed with Christ's insistent love. In celebrating the sacred story through the art of liturgical drama, the youth of the parish take part in sacramental remembering by putting flesh on the story. They claim its truths as their own, and they experience the invitation to enter a way of life and a way of worship that is ever new.

Religious Imagination

The source tool for the art of liturgical drama is the religious imagination. Imagination has led us to explore the universe, to cure disease, to contemplate God. To worship, love, and celebrate the God Jesus taught, we need a healthy religious imagination. The exercise of the religious imagination leads to faith. Our ability to believe is in direct proportion to our ability to imagine. The main tool of liturgical drama is the exercise of the religious imagination, allowing the Word to become flesh in the sacred stories we shape in the art.

Tomorrow is in the process of being imagined. As ministers and teachers, we hold the responsibility and privilege to help youth understand that they are in fact *creating* their world. What they do and who they are is infinitely significant. The decisions and choices they make today—the spiritual, physical, and intellectual foundations they are building—will support them for a lifetime and impact the next generation. The artists in a society can contribute a point of view that affects the very nature of how the past, present, and future are conceptualized. In liturgical drama we invite youth to embrace this challenge, to see themselves as central to the mission of evangelization.

The Location for Liturgical Drama

In discussions about incorporating liturgical drama, a key objection often is that liturgy should not become a performance with the congregation as spectators. I could not agree more. However, we would do well to remember that the key to creating sacred art is in the intention, commitment, gift, and craft of the person of the artist. God works through varied means to touch the hearts of humanity. The artist's intention to honor God brings a quality of immeasurable mystical value to his or her craft. This is the case whether the art is creating music, banners, or drama.

It is God who plants the seeds of creativity in the being of the artist. When the artist offers his or her life and work to the Source of All Creativity, God honors that desire. At whatever level of giftedness and craft the artist is privileged to be, when he or she intentionally connects to the Spirit, the art is elevated to the status of worship, is made holy and becomes prayer. It is this spiritual connection that is the difference between putting on a performance and participating in liturgical drama. The rest of my article deals with helping the performers understand their art as ministry.

If your troupe makes this spiritual connection, then there is little limit to where your liturgical drama can be performed. You can do liturgical drama on retreats, in religious education programs, and yes, even in sacramental liturgies. During a sacramental liturgy, liturgical drama can be done as one or more of the readings if the exact words of the Scriptures are used. It can also be done as a meditation on the readings after the homily or after Communion.

Longer dramas can be done as a complete liturgical celebration. Some parishes and schools have long histories of youth dramatizing the Passion as part of their Lenten spiritual preparation. You also may want to consider creating dramas of saints' lives and of the shorter biblical "novels"—Jonah, Ruth, Tobit, and Esther.

Sources for Liturgical Drama Scripts

Many books are available with scripts suitable for liturgical drama. I have written two books with Terri Vorndran Nichols, with icons by Vicki Shuck, called *Lectionary-Based Gospel Dramas for Advent, Christmas, and Epiphany* and *Lectionary-Based Gospel Dramas for Lent and the Easter Triduum*. They are listed in the bibliography at the end of this article, along with other resources.

The Steps in Preparing a Group

In this section I will review the steps required for forming a group of youth to perform liturgical drama. These steps work in both school and parish settings, and I have used them in both. You will need to make adaptations according to your situation, but these steps will provide the basic process.

Step 1: Calling Together a Community of Players

In forming a group of players, you may have to provide an initial motivation to convince young people to participate. I have found that this is usually easier in schools, which have some built-in motivators. For example, the high school teacher, especially the religion teacher, can make a liturgical drama a project for class or persuade students with extra credit for their participation. Teachers can also make participation in liturgical drama an option for service credit and include the use of drama and cooperative learning as a regular teaching technique.

The campus minister can gather players through her or his relationship with the other departments, especially religion, English, speech, or theater. Students can be introduced to liturgical drama as part of a peer ministry outreach or by participation in days of recollection or retreat. In relationship with parish youth ministers, students can fulfill education or service units by participating in liturgical drama.

The parish liturgist and youth coordinator may face the greatest challenges. Their love of the young people and their faith in the young people's giftedness are their most powerful draws. Of course having a youth-friendly parish in which youth are part of every ministry sets the stage for acceptance of participation in liturgical drama.

In a parish setting, liturgical drama can be offered as education or service opportunities as part of sacramental preparation for Confirmation. Peer ministry groups can embrace the art as a means of evangelization on days of recollection or retreat. A most rewarding outreach includes the formation of a teen troupe or an intergenerational group of players who offer their gifts as catechists of the Gospel in the religious education program for children and the RCIA ministries.

Step 2: Stocking Your Costume and Properties Trunk

As you gather your players, begin to fill a large trunk with costumes and props of the Bible lands. This means old choir robes, cassocks, and scarves. Even bathrobes and terry cloth towels become marvelously magical with a bit of imagination. Props remain simple: a large scroll made from construction paper or papyrus, goblets (preferably wood or metal), large cloths of various colors (especially white, black, red, and blue), plastic grapes, wheat, water pitchers, staffs, and so on. You'll begin to recognize props at garage sales and in cast-off items everywhere.

It is hoped that once you announce you are going to offer liturgical drama, people will donate generously. A costumer in the role of parent-tailor might even show up to create some actual costumes for your mission. Costumes and props need not be elaborate or detailed. There is power in simplicity, the suggestion of period. However, some costumes and props are essential. They free us to get *out* of ourselves and *into* the act.

Step 3: Preparing the Director to Empower the Players

Liturgical drama is a "poor theater." It doesn't require a large budget for sets, properties, costumes, or technical support. This organic approach to theater empowers the players to share their gifts at whatever level they are developed. Their performances are not polished or professional, but from the heart and soul of each player. In liturgical drama the players and the congregation and the story are intimately connected to one another. The drama offers player and audience a true sharing of human emotion, a sense of the timelessness of human faith—unity with the original community as well as a connection with the people gathered. The drama provides a medium through which the Word takes flesh in the Body of Christ gathered to celebrate the sacred story.

Liturgical drama requires a deep commitment from the director and performer to be a channel of the Holy Spirit. Creativity within the nature of the human spirit is an innate hunger longing to be expressed. Whoever directs the players must also be ready to minister to them, freeing them from the internal critic, teaching appreciation for the sacred story, providing an environment in which artistic expression becomes possible, teaching craft and taste, and developing the players' self-discipline.

In an organic approach to liturgical drama, the director is equally spiritual director and director of the theater arts. Within this approach the director neither designs a performance goal for the player nor communicates one. Rather the director uses prayer, meditation, theater games, and community-building techniques to draw out the natural abilities of the company. The director creates a safe and comfortable environment in which the participants trust the process enough to explore and enliven their own creativity. The director operates as a source of support and nurture, one that affirms the giftedness of each member of the troupe. Handout 1, "The

Director's Guide: Materials for Reflection," provides focus reflections to assist the director in providing this environment.

Step 4:
Spiritual Preparation for the Players—Becoming Fools for Christ

The Romans persecuted the early Christians on the stage floor of the Colosseum and the Circus. The performance of persecution was known as a spectacle, and the cross as the sign of the fool. When Saint Paul spoke to the early Christian community in Corinth, he imagined that the entire universe was watching the birth of the church. He wrote: "We have become a spectacle to the world, to angels and to mortals. We are fools for the sake of Christ" (1 Corinthians 4:9–10). The willingness to appear foolish was seen as a sign of faith. Young players today will also fight feelings of insecurity and fears of appearing foolish. They must be helped to sacrifice their shyness, vulnerability, and resistance to bond with those first followers of Jesus. We accept with dignity the title Fool for Christ.

Prayer

In preparing the players to let go of their fears and insecurities, prayer is always the first step. I offer two approaches here: the artist's prayer and the breathing mantra. However, any type of communication with the divine that offers the artist a sense of God's presence in the creative experience is the right form of prayer.

The artist's prayer can be recited individually or as a group. I find it an excellent way to begin or end a session with a group of players. You can find my version of the artist's prayer on handout 2, "The Artist's Prayer."

In the breathing mantra, you relax and center the players by helping them focus on their breathing. You can use these or similar directions:

> Quiet yourself by focusing on your breathing. Breathe slowly, filling your diaphragm with air. Exhale fully. Use your imagination to inhale the Spirit. Exhale stress. Inhale strength. Exhale insecurity. Inhale creativity. Exhale self-judgment. Inhale Jesus. Exhale fear. Breathe in God. Life is God, the source of creative energy. . . . Inhale Yahweh. Exhale stress. Inhale Elohim. Exhale insecurity. Inhale Adonai. Exhale self-judgment. Inhale Emmanuel. Exhale fear. Breathe in God . . . more God . . . Source of All . . . Source of Creative Energy.

Developing Sense Memory

After prayer the next step in the liturgical player's work is the development of sense memory—the body memory that activates feelings and produces emotions. This begins when the player takes up a script. Sense memory is rooted in the unity of *doing* and *observing*. Polishing the sense memory can be compared to a painter's preparation of the palette—supplying the emotional memory with necessary textures and colors.

To sharpen the sense memory, the director leads the players in exercises to help them absorb and take into their sense memory banks the necessary raw material that will later be woven into a performance. As the players begin each exercise, they must discipline themselves not to think about how to reproduce a certain feeling. Their only concern is to *experience* and *observe* the feeling. They must trust that when an emotion is needed for a character's development, they will find the right pathway for its expression as they attempt to apply the emotion to the lines. Once a feeling is attached to certain passages of script, the sense memory bank will automatically pour the appropriate emotion into the scene each and every time they perform.

Handout 3, "Exercises for Sense Memory," contains a number of exercises that can be used to develop the sense memory. The handout is written so that the exercises can be taken home and practiced individually, but you should also take time to do some as a group. Use these sense techniques to silence the critic. Use them in a concentrated way for a weekend retreat. Or lead the students to take one exercise each session and to work it thoroughly. Feel free to adapt and use a variety of the exercises as preparation for rehearsals and performances.

Silencing the Critic

Another crucial part of the spiritual preparation for liturgical drama is silencing the critic. In its birth process, creativity requires the absence of judgment, the silencing of the critic before it destroys what is birthing. Even as the artist begins the exercises for the stimulation of sense memory, we can hear the voice of the critic: "This is silly! What does this have to do with anything? Stop wasting your time! Go do something useful." The critic will kill the artistic impulse faster than the flu. Silence the accuser by saying, "In the name of Christ Jesus, critic be gone."

The first step in silencing the critic is to laugh at ourselves. If I laugh at myself first, then when others laugh at me, they are joining me in the joke.

This dismantles my critic and makes my insecurity part of my vocation. My self-laughter becomes part of my art.

A second step is to throw ourselves into the artistic encounter fully willing to make huge mistakes. Without permission to make garbage, there can be no art. It is critical that the privilege of making mistakes becomes a shared value when working in a cast. Every artist, regardless of his or her discipline, needs an environment where he or she can make mistakes without critical judgment from self or peer. This freedom is the environment that produces great art.

The Freak Out. Whether in writing or performing, a good way to silence the critic is to begin by jumping in like fools with no boundaries. An exercise that helps players do this is the Freak Out. All my rehearsals begin with the Freak Out. At the director's cue (I blow a whistle), the company goes wild, acts insanely. Everyone in the cast runs around screaming, moving every part of their body. At the next director's cue, silence returns to the room.

The Freak Out can be performed before or after the artist's prayer at the beginning of a rehearsal. This technique comforts and bonds a cast. It disarms feelings of foolishness. We're all fools. The real art comes later with the finding of the precious amid the chaos.

The Breath of Fire technique. The Breath of Fire technique can be used at the beginning of a rehearsal, after a break, or at any time the cast or crew is getting tired. The director leads them to follow her or him in breathing in and out as deeply as they can through the nose. The cast should begin with thirty seconds and gradually build up their stamina (without hyperventilating). This yoga technique is the fastest way I know to reach performance-level energy.

Step 5: Entering the Sacred Story—Tools for the Director

Saint Ignatius Loyola created a form of spiritual direction he called the *Spiritual Exercises*. The *Exercises* had four basic steps, or "weeks," designed to support a spiritual seeker's encounter with self and Christ: (1) contemplation of sin; (2) contemplation on the life of our Lord from his birth to Palm Sunday; (3) contemplation on the Passion of Jesus; and (4) contemplation on the Resurrection and Ascension. The following process is adapted from the *Exercises* to help the players enter into a meditation on the sacred story as preparation for character development in the drama.

Open with Prayer

The director starts by reading the Scripture passage or story that the cast intends to develop into the liturgical drama. He or she asks each player to enter a form of *lectio divina*—a process for meditating on the Scriptures. After reading the passage, each player permits a word or a phrase from the passage to demand his or her attention. The company meditates on that word or phrase on their own and then with the group. Perhaps these words will become the prayer of the day.

Explore the Story

The director suggests that the words or phrases that have been shared have a message that may take flesh in their characterization in the liturgical drama. The director leads the company in a discussion to discover the *spine*, or central message, of the passage. The spine should be able to be expressed in a single sentence. For example, the spine of the story of the rich man and Lazarus (Luke 16:19–31) might be, "It is easy for those who have much to ignore those who have little." This step is vital because it communicates the essential message that the entire company will work in unison to teach through their efforts in the liturgical drama.

Cast the Roles

Now that everyone understands the core message of the liturgical drama, it is time to cast the players in their roles. I recommend either one of two techniques: classic casting or organic casting.

In classic casting the director assigns the players their roles based on the director's insights into each player's skills and what each role requires. Classic casting works well in the beginning stages of a company's formation. However, as your troupe develops as a company, perhaps you will find organic casting more effective. An organic approach permits the casting of the scene to evolve as the players identify with different characters in the drama and help one another take on suitable roles.

The following two techniques, mind painting and discernment, can be used with either classic casting or organic casting. If you are using classic casting, use the mind-painting, faith-sharing, and discernment techniques for the rehearsal process after assigning roles.

If you are using organic casting, reserve assigning roles until after the mind-painting meditation. After the meditation the director should adapt the faith-sharing and discernment process to interpret the meaning of the group's reflections. The director should take time for prayer and discernment, both as a group and personally as director, then cast according to her or his prayerful insight. Then she or he must trust the casting decisions and continue with the work of directing.

Keep in mind that a number of players could bond with the same character during these exercises. Through discernment the director can point out that their attachment to a particular character doesn't mean that they have to play that character. (Not everyone can be Jesus.) But it may mean that they should play a role in which they are in relationship with that character. When the discernment process is entered into humbly and openly, these conflicting interests almost always work out.

Mind Painting

In the mind-painting meditation, the director invites the players to meditate on the Gospel passage or story they will later depict in the drama. The players are to *watch* the action in their mind while the director reads the story to them again very slowly. In their mind's eye they should recreate the story, imagining all the details. Mind painting is a very powerful tool, a meditation exercise wherein the players watch the scene in the sacred story unfold, noting the behaviors, feelings, and relationships of their cast character. This is an imaginative visualization that functions as a mini-rehearsal (or casting tool) while in a prayerful state.

Faith Sharing and Discernment

After the mind-painting meditation, the players should be given a few minutes to write down what they observed. Then the director facilitates a discussion around their observations, helping the players draw out the details and empowering them to recognize that the figures in the Gospels were human persons with human fears, insecurities, passions, and pride. The more the players identify with the persons in the Scriptures as real people, the more natural the characters they create will become, persons with whom both actor and audience can relate. The characters they present will become part of themselves.

In the case of a young person playing an evil character, the director should encourage the players to understand that the character erroneously believes her or his own twisted version of reality. The players need to *suspend their disbelief* for the moment and play the dysfunction as real for the sake of the Gospel. Playing a realistic Judas is a deterrent that gives the audience the opportunity to see the danger and damage an idolatrous ego can cause.

Step 6: Preparing for the Performance— Blessing the Space and Visualizations

Before each performance of the liturgical drama, it is important to claim your performance space as a holy place and to acclimate the players to it. The following are the steps I take my players through. For additional help on actually staging the liturgical drama, see handout 4, "Suggestions for Staging the Liturgical Drama."

   1. In a rehearsal space or secular theater space, the director always begins by blessing the environment. If a priest is available, he should be asked to bless the space with holy water. If not, the director and the players do the blessing by taking holy water and sprinkling it about the room, welcoming the holy angels, the saints (especially Cecilia and Genesius), and our ancestors in faith. In the name of Jesus the Christ, the company should expel the critic.

   Rehearsals held in the sanctuary of the church afford a wonderful opportunity to acknowledge the sacred space and the presence of the Eucharist and to reinforce the tradition of kneeling or bowing before Jesus present in the sacrament.

   2. Working with the cast starts with the ground beneath our feet, Mother Earth, our center and foundation. The director leads the cast to squeeze their toes in their shoes, jump and squat on the floor, make friends with the earth. To see themselves as balanced, as connected to the heavens and rooted in the earth, cast members imagine a golden chain coming down from heaven. Like a beam of golden light, the chain passes through each person and roots itself deep in the heart of Mother Earth.

   3. The director invites the guardian angels to stand beside the players on the stage. The players should visualize their angelic guardian reinforcing the truth they intend to proclaim, casting out the voice of the critic, and surrounding them with courage, wisdom, and strength. The company then calls on the Spirit (see handout 2, "The Artist's Prayer").

   4. Empowered by the love of their angel, next the players construct the boundaries of their concentration for the scene. Whether the church building or performance space is designed with a proscenium arch (a back wall and left and right wall boundaries) or a circular space, the cast needs to establish performance energy boundaries. They can do this by imagining a *fourth wall* at the perimeter of their concentration. Possibly, for realism, this boundary is in the eyes of the players. Or perhaps in their effort to reach the audience, they imagine the fourth wall as past the footlights, out into the house or congregation. My group decides each and every time where our performance concentration and boundary, or fourth wall, is placed. This is true for an individual player and for a cast. A good rule of thumb is for the players to *work,* or *throw their energy,* to the back wall of the house or church building.

Finding the balance between releasing and containing energy is the key to live performance. The energy is within the director and the company, and it permeates the sacred space. Controlling the performance energy is balancing the life force within us. We should see our performance energy coming from that golden light beam spoken of previously. This golden light becomes the energy we release and contain in our performance. We see this light passing through us to the assembly. We release this energy and accept that the Holy Spirit will decide where it travels and where it rests.

5. Just before offering the performance, the cast and crew gather in a circle and pray again for courage, strength, and the grace to communicate the sacred story. They pray that they will be channels for the spine teaching of the drama.

Depending on time this blessing ritual can be offered by cast members to cast members or by director to company. The appointed person(s) should begin by extending her or his hands over the company and giving this or a similar blessing:

> Holy Spirit, fill these players with the love and courage I see in their eyes. Christ, lead us in our sacred intention to share this drama. In the name of Jesus, I silence the critic. I place the Blessed Mother's mantle of grace around you. The Word of God takes flesh in you this day. Christ above you. Christ beside you. Christ beneath you. Christ before and behind you.

Then the director asks permission to lay hands on the players' heads or shoulders to pray for them. Or the players could do this for one another. The person doing the blessing lays hands on the head or shoulders of the player being blessed and prays silently for a moment. (If any player is uncomfortable being touched, the person performing the blessing can simply extend a hand over him or her.) Then he or she signs small crosses on the player's eyes, lips, hands, and heart, saying, "Go, proclaim the Good News to the ends of the earth."

After this blessing ritual, the director calls, "Places."

Step 7: Wrapping Up: Thanksgiving and Affirmation

After the liturgy the director meets with the players to offer thanksgiving for the honor of being able to serve, of using their gifts in the service of the Gospel. This is not the time to critique anything. The actors are too vulnerable. The director should offer only praise and thanksgiving for the gifts manifested in the players today, for the privilege of life and the gift of sharing it through art. He or she will have the opportunity to polish their performance and skills later. The players should be given time to talk about their experience over refreshments. Their nerves need to be dissipated with love and goodies. The director can affirm their courage, strength of character, and willingness to offer themselves as vehicles of the sacred story in service of the Gospel.

Finally, the director should thank the company of players, the audience, the technical crew, the person who answers the phone, the person who sweeps up, her or his partner and children. You get the idea. Thank you, God! Thank you, God! Thank you, God! Schedule the next rehearsal. Amen.

Bibliography

Theater and Drama

The following works have guided me in the development of my philosophy and technique in liturgical drama:

Barry, William A., and William J. Connolly. *The Practice of Spiritual Direction.* San Francisco: Harper and Row, 1982.

Brockett, Oscar G. *The Essential Theatre.* 2nd ed. New York: Holt, Rinehart, and Winston, 1980.

Cameron, Julia. *The Artist's Way: A Spiritual Path to Higher Creativity.* Los Angeles: Jeremy P. Tarcher/Perigee Books, 1992.

Cole, Toby, and Helen Krich Chinoy, eds. *Actors on Acting.* New rev. ed. New York: Crown Publishers, 1995.

Edwards, Tilden. *Living in the Presence: Disciplines for the Spiritual Heart.* San Francisco: Harper and Row, 1987.

Goleman, Daniel, Paul Kaufman, and Michael Ray. *The Creative Spirit.* New York: a Dutton Book, Penguin Group, 1992.

Morris, Eric. *Irreverent Acting*. New York: Putnam Publishers, 1985.

Wojtyla, Karol. *The Collected Plays and Writings on Theatre*. Trans. Boleslaw Taborski. Berkeley: University of California Press, 1987.

Sources for Liturgical Drama

O'Connell-Roussell, Sheila, and Terri Vorndran Nichols. *Lectionary-Based Gospel Dramas for Advent, Christmas, and Epiphany*. Winona, MN: Saint Mary's Press, 1997.

———. *Lectionary-Based Gospel Dramas for Lent and the Easter Triduum*. Winona, MN: Saint Mary's Press, 1999.

O'Connell-Roussell, Sheila. *The Word Is Made Flesh*. Bend, OR: Amnchara Cruces, 1997.

The Director's Guide: Materials for Reflection

The following questions have been adapted for liturgical drama from Barry and Connolly's *The Practice of Spiritual Direction*. The director should use them both as a self-reflection tool and as a tool for group reflection.

1. **How do I identify the sacred in my life?** Everything has the potential to be sacred. The goal of this question is to help the players recognize their artistic expression as a gift from God, a worthy sacrifice to be offered.

2. **Am I unafraid of life?** People may have fears related to participation in liturgical drama. Owning the fear dissipates its influence. We sacrifice and make holy our insecurity for the sake of the Gospel.

3. **Am I in relationship with the God who has loved first?** Seeing ourselves as loved and valuable, as competent, and as worthy and able is the source of performance ability. God is the source. Self-consciousness is dissipated by the consciousness of the sacred message we want to share.

4. **Do I have a deep desire to help myself and others communicate with God?** to celebrate the mystery of life? The performer gives of one's self. The goal of the art form is communication. The artist's deepest performance desire is to focus all of one's energies, ability, and spirit on the message communicated.

5. **Am I trustworthy in cherishing and protecting the confidentiality of another's journey?** Sharing one's faith journey and questions are important in preparing for liturgical drama. This also makes players vulnerable to one another. Criticism and gossip can be devastating. Members of the troupe must commit to confidentiality surrounding the personal soul searching shared in the company.

6. **Am I able to hear another's story without judgment?** All players require a safe environment in which to grow. All actors and technical members commit to being ministers of listening with caring compassion. When one actor is judged, the whole company feels so. Humor has a high value in the group's journey together; however, it must be clear that ridicule of another's feelings or experiences is outlawed. Mockery is very different from healthy humor.

7. Am I able to look at my own journey without judgment? Players discover that the most severe judge is the internal critic. Performance art is a living art form. It takes place in the present moment. We must silence the internal critic.

8. Am I committed to the communal good more than my own ego? Liturgical drama, like all organic theater projects, rejects all "star" players. All members of the troupe are equal and valuable. The actor is as important as the member who organizes the props. The "striking of the set," or cleanup, is as needed as the performance. We are a company of players, a community dedicated to equality before our God.

9. How do I communicate my own spiritual journey? Communicating the transcendent is difficult; putting language to religious experience is challenging. Symbol, ritual, and drama are needed to communicate the sacred. The members of the company dedicate themselves as catechists, using artistic language to communicate the holy.

10. What happens to me as I pray? Prayer is the appropriate manner in which to offer one's performance. Becoming conscious of the source within, the spirit of God, is the ground on which to stand as we offer ourselves as media for the sacred story.

The Artist's Prayer

I surround myself with the Source of Creativity, the light of the Holy Spirit. Christ, enter with your truth. Journey with me into each memory, each feeling and emotion. Heal my fear and woundedness. Make me aware of your presence. I long to live within your will, to make choices that will empower me to become conscious of who God created me to be, your design for my life and for the world you created.

Come, Holy Spirit, be my teacher. Fill me with your compassion. I accept whatever information I need for my growth, for the empowerment of my art and craft, for my correction and education, for the betterment of those whom you gather as audience. I humbly offer myself as clay for your sculpting. I offer myself as a channel of your grace, your wisdom. Use my body, my voice, and my mind and will to teach your truth.

Spirit of Wisdom, Ancient Storyteller, speak through me. I offer myself as your channel. Guide me in this journey into self as I humbly portray your holy message through my art. Surround my drama partners and me with your holy defending angels to protect us against the voice of the critic—whether within or without us. Fill this company with strength and courage, with stamina and joy for the privilege of performing. Bless those who join us for the drama.

Lord Jesus, may we see with your eyes, feel with your sacred heart. Creator, Redeemer, Sanctifier, bless our performance with your presence. Be our witness and partner in this art. We invoke the prayers of Saint Cecilia, patron of music, and Saint Genesius, patron of theater, to bless our efforts and to stand beside us in the liturgical drama. We offer ourselves in this work so that all may come to know the love of God. We acknowledge Christ above us, Christ beside us, Christ beneath and within us. We bless ourselves in the name of our Creator, Redeemer, and Sanctifier. Amen.

Exercises for Sense Memory

1. Read a Scripture passage. Relish each word in your mind, identify each word's meaning.
2. Be aware of your desire *to perform* within God's will. See yourself "floating on the sea of God's will." See yourself as a lump of clay in the hands of the Creator. Concentrate on your senses: seeing, hearing, feeling, smelling, and tasting. Tell God how it feels to be in the divine hands, re-created as the Holy One wills.
3. Surrender yourself to the Source as an act of faith. Release all resistance. Offer your gifts and failings in open, trusting awareness of the Spirit's presence in the creative process. Invite the Spirit to pray through you.
4. Remember the details of the day, the clothes you wore, the people you encountered. Remember sounds, smells, colors, and textures. Discipline yourself to make a habit of absorbing sensory stimuli toward the permanent expansion of your consciousness.
5. Remember a colorful and emotional event—a special anniversary, birthday, or holiday. Go there in your mind. Identify and call on the emotions from that day. Was this an experience of warmth or a black hole in your mind? Remember. Remember.
6. Sit in silence until you can feel the blood rushing through your veins. Listen to the beating of your own heart. See your blood as a river of living water nourishing the seed of new life that God has planted within you. See your creative impulses at the very root of your person being watered by the Divine One. Commit to the interior change that this growth will bring.
7. Let people and situations spontaneously rise to your awareness. Offer them to God, remembering how limited our vision is. God's ultimate understanding of all situations holds the truth of all experiences. Pray for whomever comes to mind.
8. Transmit blessings to someone; see her or him surrounded with the love of the Spirit. See healing energy encircle that person as you bless her or him with happiness. Note your ability to send and throw this sacred energy. Throwing energy is the key to performance.

Exercises for Sense Memory 2

9. Recall your most recent experience of anger. For the sake of character development, try to justify your experience and understand the emotion. Feel it. Release it to God. Remember a variety of other strong emotional experiences and apply the above technique to each. Repeat! Repeat! Repeat! Release them to God.
10. Will yourself to remain in a good or bad mood for a certain definite period. Gradually increase the minutes or hours. Notice your body, your voice, and your energy. Take a walk. Discipline yourself to be aware of all sounds and events in the environment. Notice all details. Be aware of how they make you feel.
11. Study a person and try to analyze his or her mood. Notice body changes for various moods, tone and texture of the voice, breathing, posture, and so on. Imitate what you see.
12. Work for hours and hours before a mirror studying your face. Change the mood and notice the muscles and every nuance of emotional response. This cannot be overdone. Learn your own face—how it looks and how it feels in various emotional states.
13. Silence the critic. Address the accuser: "You are not permitted to speak! Christ is before me! Christ is behind me! Christ is beneath me! Christ is above me! Spirit, fill me with your presence. Protect me from the demon of criticism."
14. Close your exercise in prayer. Commit your craft to God. Pray that we artists may be given the privilege of contributing to the healing of self, others, and the earth. Pray in thanksgiving when you finish.

Suggestions for Staging the Liturgical Drama

1. There is minimal theater illusion created in this type of performance. The players are aware of the audience, and the audience is repeatedly made aware that they are not unseen spectators. We watch and respond in the *now*.
2. The fourth wall, which permits the "magic if" (the permission the audience gives the player to create another reality) to take place, goes up when dramatic realism is desired to capture a private natural exchange. The fourth wall can be projected to include the back wall of the performing space in order to draw the audience into the scene as players. Or the boundary can be removed entirely to bring the audience into the story to such a degree that the issue in the art demands a response. Fourth wall manipulation is a powerful device.
3. Asides to the audience are employed as an alienation device, even to the extent of breaking the characterization to destroy illusion and remind the audience that we are performing here.
4. Use of liturgical garments and sacred objects to symbolize the connection between the character portrayed or narrated and the modern-day sacramental association creates sacred space.
5. Changing character and scene props in front of the audience and using ritual, mask, gesture, costume, and dramatized (even memorized and performed) readings of the script from the lectern result in both performer self-alienation and audience distancing—which are both important in distinguishing liturgical drama from entertainment. These techniques help the audience connect with the greater narrative.
6. Containing the audience applause is another important audience-distancing technique for liturgical drama. Whenever there is an obvious break in the action, a place where the audience thinks it should applaud, we move in liquid ritual, continuing the drama to prevent the catharsis of applause. This alienation technique and manipulation of performance energy has the effect of containing the audience's reaction. By the end of the act they are ready to explode emotionally, resulting in a powerful emotional concentration on your story's content.

Handout 4: Permission to reproduce this handout for program use is granted.

Suggestions for Staging the Liturgical Drama 2

7. Secondary and chorus characters can be developed using alienation devices as part of their presentation of self. The use of hand props, costume changes in view of the audience, and masks and technical equipment on stage all break the emotional paradigm. Alienation devices offer teaching moments in which the playwrights offer their moral cloaked in stagecraft and assessable without preaching.

With minimal sets, costumes, and properties, liturgical drama blends representational and presentational theater with elements of performance art, liturgical drama, and Greek chorus. The fourth wall goes up and down from scene to scene throughout the Gospel or morality play. Different characters tell their story from the point of view of the past or take us into the world of their memory to let us experience the event as the character experienced it in the present moment.

To empower player and audience to remember that we are chosen children of God, do not focus on creating a realistic historical reconstruction of the period. Rather create a path of conversion. With each performance it is our prayer that we all will be more aware of the presence of the Spirit in our midst and of who we are called to be as followers of Jesus.

Vibrant Multicultural Liturgy:
Saint Michael's Story

Tom Heinen and C. J. Hribal

Tom Heinen is the religion reporter for the *Milwaukee Journal Sentinel*. C. J. Hribal is a novelist and associate professor of English at Marquette University. Both are members and lay leaders at Saint Michael's Parish in Milwaukee, Wisconsin. This article is based on their parish experience and interviews with parish ministers and parish youth.

Led by a young person carrying a streaming banner of red and white ribbons atop a processional pole, adult celebrants and children flow down the main aisle of Saint Michael's Church in Milwaukee. The words "We are one, we are one, we are one in the Spirit" arise from a mixed choir of Asians, Hispanics, African Americans and Anglos—both young people and adults—standing on risers behind the altar.

Younger children, some of them middle school age, fan out along the front of the broad altar platform and use choreographed sign language to convey the lyrics to the multicultural congregation. Many people in the pews sing. Many also join in the sign language, at one point forming interlocking circles with their thumbs and forefingers for the words "We are one."

It is Pentecost, and before the service is over, several different tongues are indeed spoken in readings, prayers, and songs that range from traditional to hand-clapping Gospel and pulsating Latino. The words and rhythms rise and resonate off the vaulted ceilings, carved triptych, and Austrian stained-glass windows of a landmark neo-Gothic church that was built in 1892 to serve German immigrants.

To Sr. Carmelita Deanda, a South American nun who works with Hispanic young people at Saint Michael's, the blending of cultures at the parish is a gift from God. During conversations she raises one hand and then the other to represent different ethnic groups.

"Not only this community or this one, but everyone," she exclaims in accented English. "We can show other parishes how we can come together. I think it's beautiful. A gift. There's a feeling of, 'I can give something to them, and they can give something to me.'"

A Changing Parish

The congregation at Saint Michael's today is much different from the German-speaking congregation of the late 1800s. But the parish's mission has returned to its roots.

In its current rebirth, Saint Michael's serves as a gateway into U.S. society for first- and second-generation immigrants from several non-European countries. Parishioners and neighborhood residents get help with anything from school tutoring to immigration law requirements. There is a parish nurse. A housing program run out of the parish rectory has stabilized families and neighborhoods by helping four hundred first-time homeowners buy houses in the area around the church, with only a single foreclosure.

Saint Michael's is also a gateway to the Catholic church. Many of its over 1,050 Asian members converted to Catholicism from Buddhism or animism after being attracted to the parish because its mix of ethnic liturgies, social services, and openness to newcomers gave them a warm home in an otherwise foreign, urban landscape.

The issue of how to involve children and young people in liturgies and parish life is critical here. Many of the Asians in particular have large families. Of the nearly 1,900 registered parishioners, 33 percent are age thirteen or younger, and 43 percent are age seventeen or younger. The actual numbers are probably higher because some people are reluctant to register with any church or government agency.

What's more, Saint Michael's is collaborating closely with two other central-city Milwaukee parishes that have significant numbers of Hispanics or African Americans: Saint Rose and Saint Francis. The Pentecost service is a tri-parish service, though all the ethnic groups are represented among Saint Michael's registered congregation of 649 Hispanics, 613 Hmong tribal people from Laos, 439 Laotians, 128 Anglo-Americans, and 68 African Americans.

Today the main Sunday Mass at 9 a.m. is a multicultural liturgy in three languages—Lao, Hmong, and English. A noon Mass in Spanish (and sometimes also in English) serves most of the Hispanics. The communities come together for a Mass in four languages on major feast days, often with members of Saint Rose and Saint Francis as well. And once a month there is also a separate Mass for the Hmong.

Engaging Youth in Liturgy

The answer to the question of how to engage young people in liturgy, especially in one of the most multicultural parishes in the ten-county Archdiocese of Milwaukee, is a work in progress. Saint Michael's has had significant successes. Like many parishes, it also is struggling. It has not found surefire steps for overcoming yawning disinterest, rebellious skepticism, or empty alienation. However, current and former pastoral teams have done several things to help make the church and its liturgies a meaningful part of teenagers' lives. The following strategies can make teenagers and preteens feel part of the services:

- Have costumed children and teenagers act out the Gospel message while adults or older teens read. This is done for Palm Sunday, Good Friday, Christmas Eve, and other special occasions, such as the Hispanic feast day of Our Lady of Guadalupe. On the feast of Saint Michael, young people in an Asian dragon costume come roaring down the center aisle to the front of the sanctuary, where a line of younger children holding a long, thick, golden-tipped pole "slay" the dragon, as the lector reads how Saint Michael triumphed over evil.
- Involve children, young people, and adults together on a regular basis in a wide-ranging music ministry. Saint Michael's has a children's choir, a predominantly African American gospel choir, an Asian choir, and a general choir. A youth choir exclusively for older teens is being considered. A variety of student musicians playing anything from keyboard and violin to saxophone and harp give solo and duet performances each Christmas Eve before, and sometimes during, the Mass.
- Have younger boys and girls, often in multiethnic teams, serve as acolytes at each Mass. The schedule rotates frequently to get as many children as possible involved and to impress on them that it is a privilege. This keeps some engaged through their middle school years. This and other measures also help provide a visual message to children and young people that their ethnic groups and age-groups are an important part of what is taking place.
- Invite skilled middle school and high school students to serve regularly as readers and song leaders in rotation with adults. Songs and readings are presented in different languages, usually with translations available. The young people are much more comfortable speaking English, and the Asian young people often can't read their parents' language in the native script. But the blending of languages and other cultural elements into liturgies provides an underlying sense of familiarity that makes both the parents and the young people feel comfortable. And immigrant parents in particular are proud to see their children take active roles in liturgies.
- Periodically have children and young people bring the offertory gifts to the altar. This includes the Laotians' practice of *boun*

(pronounced boon)—an adaptation of their Buddhist tradition of bringing gifts to the monks. Silver bowls containing anything from fruit and crackers to incense sticks and soap are placed on the floor in front of the altar during the offertory in thanks for answered prayers or as a memorial on the anniversary of the death of a loved one. "Money trees"—branches with paper currency attached to them—are also given.
- Occasionally have young people serve as ushers and hospitality ministers.

These are just a few pieces of a larger mosaic in which the overall image—a warm, family-friendly environment in which each ethnic group sees some of its own culture while feeling part of a larger whole—is more important than any of the individual parts.

People have a variety of perspectives on this unity in diversity. The most fundamental one seems to be that many parishioners have learned to like the mix of cultures, and that blend within the context of liturgy is an attraction for all age-groups, especially young people.

Blong Yang, the parish's Hmong deacon, says that Hmong families now generally prefer to have multicultural liturgies. In the Hmong tradition, a person cannot be neutral in spiritual matters. One must believe in something and participate, in this case by attending church services, Blong says. And wherever the adults go to participate, they bring their children. The difficulty is that the young people often are trying to blend into U.S. society, so they generally do not read or write in Hmong and have trouble following readings at exclusively Hmong services. The parents, on the other hand, often struggle with the English language and with the dominant U.S. culture. They want to see their own culture reflected in the services, and they fear that their children will become so assimilated that they will lose much of their cultural identity. Multicultural liturgies meet the entire family's needs and thereby create a bridge between the generations.

This also is true for the Laotians, says Sr. Alice Thepouthay, a member of the Sisters of Charity of Saint Joan Antida and the pastoral staff member who works with Laotians. Having traveled to many parishes around the country as a consultant in Laotian ministry, Sister Alice believes that Saint Michael's is unusual, perhaps unique. Other parishes Sister Alice has visited are just now moving toward celebrating the kinds of multiethnic liturgy that Saint Michael's has embraced for nearly two decades. Instead of having separate liturgies for Laotians, the parish has a blended liturgy. She and other parish staff members see this as the cornerstone of Saint Michael's success.

"I think people continue to come, even if they don't understand a lot of the service, because some of the Scripture readings are in their own language, some of the music is in their own language, some of the people in the ministries are from their communities," says Fr. Dennis Lewis, who has been pastor of Saint Michael's for eleven years. "They are participants. Not the whole, but there is always a role for them to play, and a role that brings understanding to them as part of that whole. And I think that's what's attractive. And I think there is an overall sense that when there is that larger community that gathers, there's something missing if that larger community isn't there. If it's just one segment of the community, they have come to realize that something's missing, that spirituality of the whole is more important than spirituality of the part."

Why Do They Keep Coming?

It would be wonderful to claim that the multicultural liturgies celebrated at Saint Michael's keep all the parish youth involved and connected, but it would not be true. As in other churches, a significant number of young people drift away from participation in Saint Michael's liturgies as they grow older. But others stay, offering insight and hope. Why do they keep coming?

"Sunday worship for our young people is truly a belonging opportunity," says Father Dennis, who for the past two years has served as pastor of both Saint Michael's and Saint Rose's. "As much as they say they are iconoclasts and everything else, they want to belong. And it gives them a safe belonging, a group belonging for good that goes beyond mom and dad.

"One thing we're able to offer them is other adult mentors who aren't part of their ethnic community. The first thing the Hmong youth complain about is, 'Oh, the elders or our parents want us to do it this way.' And so they'll actively look to another adult who is not part of their community. And parents affirm this because they trust in the church."

Sunday Mass also offers young people a chance to socialize. "They usually come because, first thing, they like to see some of their friends," says Deacon Blong. Although more needs to be done to bring different ethnic youth groups in the parish together, coming to church on Sunday also offers young people an opportunity to get to know people their age from different cultures.

"I really do believe this," Father Dennis says. "When they go to the public school systems—and they're defenseless, and they don't have parents backing them up, and they're in there for survival—they sit at their lunch tables with their own groups and everything falls apart again. But here on Sundays, I've seen kids identifying with kids from other communities."

"It has something to do with the culture of that room when we are all there together," says Barbara Tracey, the parish liturgy director and music coordinator. "We are not a stiff, formal assembly. If you've got an announcement, you can get up and make it. And if you're a kid and you want to get up and make an announcement, you don't have to clear that with a whole bunch of people ahead of time."

Sister Alice observes: "We're more like family. The young children feel so happy to come to church." She cites the various activities and roles in which the children are included and grow into as they get older. "There's an enthusiasm," she says, "to do something in the church." Certainly as they become teens they come to church less often—perhaps twice a month rather than every week—but she observes that they do come again more frequently as they marry and have children. "They don't lose faith, they just come less often. They come back when they've settled down because they feel comfortable here," she says.

Even the youngest children feel a part of the community at Mass. There is no cry room. There are no restricted areas where children and young people must or must not sit. Sometimes small children will wander down an aisle or totter in front of the altar platform. Bemused parishioners look on as though the children were nephews, nieces, and grandchildren at a family gathering. Eventually they are retrieved by parents. Because of the large numbers of very young children, there is often an undercurrent of noise—what Tracey refers to as a kind of constant hubbub. People are free to shush misbehaving children, but the immigrant populations are comfortable allowing some of the normal energy of family life to flow into the church.

Saint Michael's Keys for Multicultural Liturgy

In *From Age to Age: The Challenge of Worship with Adolescents,* the third goal calls liturgy planners to attend to the diversity of ages and cultures in the assembly. This section of the paper states: "The rites need to reflect this diversity of cultures by examples, musical styles, decor, and references to current events. *We feel ourselves called to reach out beyond our nationalities, races, languages and socio-economic levels, so as to be really one Catholic family"* (no. 55). Through trial and error, and openness to experimentation, the staff at Saint Michael's has developed liturgies that respond to this challenge and continue to evolve.

One thing the parish staff discovered is that a multicultural Mass at Saint Michael's does not take much longer than a single-language liturgy. The length is controlled by selectively incorporating the languages of each of the ethnic groups in the service rather than translating everything for everyone. Father Dennis explains, "You don't repeat in the languages over and over and over again, but you certainly provide the alternative, either written or otherwise, so that people can understand where they are, what the Scripture lesson is for that day, without having three readers read the first reading, three readers read the second reading." Typically one of the readings at the 9 a.m. Mass is in Lao or Hmong, and the English speakers follow along in their missalette. The other reading is in English. There are also Spanish missalettes for Hispanic Masses and combined liturgies.

Songs, too, are sung in the different languages. Through the various choirs and the parish's specially prepared songbooks, music has been a major force in getting young people and adults involved as participants rather than observers. Music reflects ethnic culture. And the blend of traditional hymns and lively, upbeat songs adds a variety that both energizes and inspires. Everyone claps their hands when the gospel choir sings or when Latino musicians bring their amplified guitars and drums to a combined liturgy.

One key to the success of the music program has been the creation of songbooks that enable people to understand and sing along even if they don't speak or read another language. Many songs are not only offered in two or three languages on facing pages, but there are also phonetic pronunciation guides so that, for example, an English-speaking person can join the Asians in singing a song in Lao or Hmong. And sometimes people are encouraged to sing the same song in whatever language they prefer, simultaneously.

Barbara Tracey feels strongly that there be a single hymnal with many of the songs available in the various languages. "That's the thing," Tracey says, "not having a bunch of books in your pews where it's all segmented.

The idea is that we're pulling them all together into one book. It speaks of our community, of how we all fit together." For many of the songs, Tracey worked with Deacon Blong to translate the English songs into Hmong. She's done the same thing with the English-Lao songs, with a phonetic translation appearing below the Lao script for English speakers. Getting copyright approval is time consuming, but a number of commercially available software programs ease the task of preparing the pages for music directors who would like to do the same thing with their parish hymnal. The multiethnic nature of Saint Michael's shows up in the liturgy in other ways as well, from the *boun* offerings, to the lighting of long incense sticks on the altar at the start of most Masses, to the incorporation of such gestures as bowing, and to the blessing by the priest or eucharistic ministers of young children accompanying their parents during Communion.

The mix of music, drama, ethnic touches, and spontaneous announcements gives liturgies and other church events a stability and unpredictability that reflect some of the dynamics of people's lives. "Boy, you never know what you're going to see," says one parishioner. And for young people, that can be a plus.

"I don't know if it's just the music," Tracey says. "There's always something different going on, you know. They're not just sitting there looking at the backs of people's heads, because there are little kids moving around, and different languages to hear, and different songs. All of that, I think, probably contributes to not getting bored. There's a sense of spontaneity." Adds Father Dennis, "There's a sameness to the form, but there's a spontaneity within the form that prevents them from being bored."

One way the youth manage to avoid boredom is by becoming involved in the liturgy itself; a number of them participate in the ways outlined earlier in this article. And rather than segregate them by age, by having a youth Mass, their participation is blended into every service at Saint Michael's. More important, their participation extends beyond liturgy and into the life of the parish itself. Individual groups and activities reach some of the young people at Saint Michael's and at Saint Francis and Saint Rose. But many more could participate, and one ethnic group's youth activities don't often extend to other ethnic groups. Plans are under way now for a tri-parish, multicultural youth group, says Shanedra Johnson, an African American woman who began in August of 1998 as tri-parish pastoral associate for African American ministry and added the job of tri-parish youth minister in January of 1999.

"Youth need to interact more than just when they're in church," says Johnson, a longtime member of Saint Michael's. "We want them to get to know each other cross-parish. They'll work together, learn about other cultures, but also learn more about church."

A Spirit of Openness

Another key element of Saint Michael's success is that liturgies have a comfortable, homelike atmosphere. There is a blend of sacred formality and easygoing informality. That's best evidenced during Mass at the exchange of peace, when many people leave their pews, embrace, or exchange greetings and handshakes with others from many ethnic backgrounds and age-groups. No one knows how long it would go on if the priest didn't return to the altar and continue the liturgy.

That exchange is symbolic of the parish's welcoming spirit. And it is that spirit that has both attracted minorities and created a sense of home for them.

Hispanics have been members at Saint Michael's for decades, though their numbers are growing more rapidly now with new immigrants from Mexico. The parish has had few African American members, but the closing of some other central-city parishes in recent years has brought them to Saint Michael's in increasing numbers, too. Now a local chapter of the Knights and Ladies of Saint Peter Claver meets regularly in the church for Sunday Mass, and some of its members have become active parishioners.

The spirit of openness that welcomes African Americans to Saint Michael's today goes back nearly twenty years. Hmong people came to the parish in 1982, and Laotians came in 1984, at a time when deteriorating neighborhoods, shifting demographics, and declining numbers of Anglos were putting the future of the parish in doubt. The Asians, then two small groups with a few families each, were looking for a home church in which they would be accepted and have room to grow. The parishioners who remained at Saint Michael's had learned to accept change. They and the pastoral team at that time quickly embraced the Asian newcomers.

"Most of the people at Saint Michael's were converted here," Sister Alice says of the Laotians. "Saint Michael's is like a home for them. They don't need to call me. They just walk in the door because they see my car outside. It is a village. They consider themselves like, 'our country.' I never tell them, 'There is not time. I cannot see you.' I try to do the best I can to make them feel at home."

Was there something special that enabled this to happen at Saint Michael's? "I think the openness of Saint Michael's is amazing," Sister Alice adds. "It's amazing to see black, yellow, white together. Even the old folk, the senior people, they never complain. I'm traveling for six, seven years all over this country. A lot of people don't accept them [Laotians] as they are. You know, instead of talking with them, they criticize them behind their back. When the Hmong people heard about that, they had hurt feelings. . . . Saint Michael's is special because we are very, very open. Not only for the Laotian, for anyone of any ethnic group to come to our place."

Contributing to members' feeling that "this is our place" was a major renovation and cleaning of the cavernous upper church, which was similar to a Works Progress Administration program. Parishioners, many of them poor and jobless, were employed by the parish to do the work. They stripped and refinished all the pews and woodwork; disassembled, cleaned, and gilded the ornately carved back and side altars; constructed the central front altar (including delicate wood cuttings) and its platform; and painted the church's entire interior. This gave the parishioners a tremendous sense of belonging and ownership.

The Wisdom of Young People

Saint Michael's success in bringing people of diverse cultures together has been hard fought. One key is a willingness to listen to the stories and needs of each culture. There is now a growing awareness that the parish needs to listen to young people in the same way. Ultimately, even when they don't realize it, teens themselves hold the answers to the question of how to get youth more involved in the spiritual and social life of the church. Each youth has a story to tell and wisdom to share. Here are a few of those perspectives:

Juan Silver

Juan Silver, age sixteen, has been a member of the Hands of Jesus—a Hispanic youth group—for about a year. "My parents thought it was a good idea. I wasn't sure. But now it's comforting being in the group. If you dress a certain way, people have a certain idea of you. But here people accept you for who you are. If you have a problem, there are kids to talk to who understand what you're going through. It's a good group. It keeps us off the streets and gives us something to look forward to. I decided to make it a commitment. There are people out there who need help, and if you can offer it to them, that's a good thing to do."

Lydia Sanchez

Lydia Sanchez, age eighteen, has been a member of the Hands of Jesus for two and a half years. "I wanted to be more active at church. It's like a second family. Everybody feels really comfortable with everybody else. We're all helping each other out. Each of us has gone through some of the same things. It's something different to do than just hanging out with your friends or your family. It makes me want to go to church more. Because of Saint Michael's multicultural liturgy," she says, "we learn how other people do things. We're praising the same God, but in different languages. It's amazing. We all get together, and you forget that he's Mexican or he's Hmong. I mean, we're different, we have these different languages, but we're all doing the same thing in these different languages." Having parish-wide potlucks and social get-togethers after some Masses increases that feeling of community. "We exchange food, we taste one another's food, and we're exchanging culture, too."

Phensy Vatsana

Phensy Vatsana, age eighteen, has been a lector since she was thirteen. She's also a leader in a recently formed Laotian youth group. Like Lydia, she wanted to be more active at church. "I wanted to try something new. I wanted to take part in Mass, not just sit there." She thinks it's great that altar servers and choir members are now actively recruited from the ranks of younger kids. "They're excited. It's awesome to see them excited. It gives them a start. Kids swing this way and that. Saint Michael's helps them swing the right way." Helping kids "swing the right way" is what is behind her helping start the Laotian youth group. Most in the group are teens, and they want to help younger kids—kids in middle school and the primary grades—with things like homework, tutoring, and getting them to think about careers. "We want this to be a big brother–big sister kind of relation-ship, where you know them more than just to say 'hi' when you see them. You make them feel like family, know what's going on in their family." The number one thing Phensy wants the kids to realize is, "Education takes you everywhere. Education and school." That education continues at Saint Michael's. She thinks having young people participate in the Mass is good for the other young people to see. "It makes it more interesting for them.

Kids go, 'Wow, who's up there?' You're their age, or maybe a little older—somebody they look up to. It's not just a bunch of adults." It helps her, too. For her the multicultural aspect of the liturgy is important. "We appreciate other people's language and culture. Having the readings in different languages, and at Pentecost having all the readings in all the languages, we learn that ours isn't the only culture, that one doesn't just dominate."

Shoua Hue

Shoua Hue, age twenty, was elected president of the nearly twenty-member Hmong youth group of Saint Michael's in 1999. She came to Milwaukee and Saint Michael's from California in July of 1996. Her West Coast church had exclusively Hmong services. She cares about her faith but found that she was not attending Mass regularly until she got involved with the Hmong youth group at Saint Michael's. "I'll admit that I wasn't much into going to church before, but because I got involved these past couple of years with the youth and have become better friends with them, they make me want to attend church and learn a little bit more," says Shoua, now a sales associate and processing assistant at a large Milwaukee-based bank. "Not only do we learn about God, but we also go to Mass because we learn about each other. And then, you know, we learn about each other's faith in God as well."

Shoua thinks that many Hmong youth and young adults still attend church when they can. Because many have full- or part-time jobs, the only time most of them can get together is on Sundays after Mass. "I know that there are some who hardly ever get to Mass because of their work schedule," she said. "I know that a lot of them, they do come to pray. It's not that they come just because we call for a meeting. They do have faith in God, and that's what they do come for, to pray. A lot of them are driving themselves to church, so it's their own decision to go." The Hmong youth apparently like the multicultural liturgies and the music, but she says that they need to find ways to get more help. "They need someone to explain and help them understand the wording, because for them to just sit through Mass and listen, a lot of the time they get restless and stuff, and then they start talking," she said. "I feel we should get together and discuss exactly what's going on in the readings."

Tracy Davis

Tracy Davis, age sixteen, has been at Saint Michael's for her entire life. An African American, she sings in the gospel choir and the general choir.

"When I come, when I sing, whatever mood I'm in, it makes me feel better," she says. "People give me confidence. They tell me to keep trying, to keep singing, to keep striving for my goals. It's just like a big old support system. Sometimes it's boring, but when we get a chance to plan and to sing, it's fine."

Orlando Diaz

Orlando Diaz, age eighteen, has been a member of Saint Francis Church all his life, but he has friends at Saint Michael's because the parishes' choirs sing together and because he's participated in other activities with Saint Michael's young people. He knows Tracy Davis because they both are choir members, and both have taken part in a youth leadership program at the House of Peace, an outreach ministry run by the Capuchins in a neighborhood between the two parishes. "It [Mass] is meaningful for me because there are a lot of things that are missing out of the week, out of everyday life," Orlando says. "You all get together and you have time to realize there are things greater than yourself." He adds, "I'd say it's the community, just having everybody here. Teenagers, we tend to be very socially oriented, and this is a good place to be together with people your age and with people not your age." What do teens like about the multicultural liturgies? "One thing is the music," he says. "We do like music, and that's no secret. And so if you can have more upbeat music, that will involve the youth. If you can walk by the church and hear the music, that will draw youth."

These comments from the young people of our parish best express the successes and the challenges we face at Saint Michael's. We have learned much about bringing people from different cultures together, but we still face many struggles, particularly with our youth. As a work in progress we continue to press forward in faith, believing that God will bless our efforts to welcome all people. May our story be an inspiration and a model to others to embrace and celebrate our wonderful diversity as the people of God.

To contact the staff who has developed this multicultural liturgy and who work with these young people, you can e-mail the parish at stmike@execpc.com *or write Saint Michael's Parish, 1445 N. 24th Street, Milwaukee, WI 53205.*

Youth and Liturgy:
A Hispanic Perspective

Peter M. Kolar

Peter Kolar is a composer and arranger, the editor of Hispanic music and publications for World Library Publications, and a music director at Holy Cross/IHM Parish in Chicago. Besides directing the parish children's and youth choirs, he leads the Holy Cross/IHM Marimba Ensemble, composed of inner-city Hispanic youth.

I like to imagine that the church is like an airport terminal: the different arrival and departure gates represent the church's different ministries: liturgy, theology, music, youth, and so on. Add into the picture another culture and language (like Hispanic culture and Spanish language), and it's like building another complete terminal with its own set of gates: *Hispanic* liturgy, *Hispanic* theology, *Hispanic* music, and so on. If you traveled through the old terminal regularly, you would be accustomed to its layout and function. But on entering this new terminal for the first time, you would have to start all over in getting acquainted with it. For those who enjoy the possibilities of exploration, this poses a new adventure, but for many, the natural reaction to unfamiliarity is fear.

Hispanic ministry, like youth ministry, is a new frontier. And some people are afraid because they are unfamiliar with the territory. In this article I will provide you with some "signs" to help you become more familiar with this territory. I hope to help you become excited and perhaps a little less fearful about ministering with Hispanic youth. As you are probably aware, the cultural landscape of the U.S. Catholic church is changing rapidly. Awareness of this has brought about a major focus on both Hispanic ministry and youth ministry. When you put these two ministries together, someone working in Hispanic youth ministry has their hands full!

Personal Motivations

My own journey into Hispanic ministry was more than just a vocational decision, it was a personal one. I am of Hispanic descent—my mother is from El Salvador—but my upbringing was very Anglo. Therefore this journey has been a personal one of rediscovering the Hispanic culture. I have had to incur many of the reality checks that an outsider to Hispanic culture might have when becoming acquainted with it. I have loved what I have seen and learned; I have at last become a part of the culture, and that which was missing before has finally become part of me. I invite others to take the journey also.

As for ministry, I have been involved in the church since my childhood—specifically through music. I am a musician, and it was through music that I was first invited to serve in my parish as a child and as a youth. Now as an adult I work with youth in a Spanish-speaking Mexican community through a parish music program. As it is often said, I probably have learned just as much from the young people about life as they have from me about music—because my ministry has extended far beyond my duties in just music. More important, I have learned that to work with youth—specifically Hispanic youth—requires a great deal of patience, understanding, and creativity, but that the rewards are more than gratifying. I hope that sharing my experiences enlightens, affirms, and inspires those who have an interest in this ministry.

Ministry with Hispanic Youth

For Hispanic people, worship is closely tied to their experience of community. Positive experiences of the church in their daily lives make for authentic celebration during liturgy. Therefore I want to begin by talking about ministry with Hispanic youth in general before talking specifically about what makes for vibrant liturgy with Hispanic young people.

Today's Hispanic Youth: The Adolescent Search for Identity

Working with Hispanic youth requires keeping two things in mind: they are *Latino* (a term used synonymously with *Hispanic*), and they are *American*. We like to have convenient terms that lump everything together, like *Mexican American* or *Latin American,* but this kind of terminology neglects a very basic dichotomy in the life of every Hispanic who resides in the United States: the struggle for identity. For instance, what are the influences of popular U.S. culture that have infiltrated the Hispanic way of thinking? And how is the Hispanic adolescent similar to a typical "American" teen? On the other hand, what are the cultural elements that make a Latino youth's life different from that of a typical "American" teen? What Hispanic traditions may have been lost?

Keep in mind that according to U.S. Census Bureau statistics and projections, it won't be long before the "typical" American youth will be of non-Anglo, non-Euro-American descent. So perhaps the more relevant question might be, How will Hispanic culture influence the typical American lifestyle in the years to come? (Already the most popular name among newborn males in many states is José, not John, Michael, or David.)

Latino or American?

In ministering with Hispanic youth, there is a certain surface level that does not require dealing with a lot of Hispanic issues. Today's typical Latino youth are more integrated into mainstream culture than any other generation; issues of racism, social class, and language barriers do not come into play as much as they would have a generation earlier. That is to say, most Hispanic youth are typical American youth—when it comes to popular music, clothes, sports, fads, and so on. Hispanic youth, like most adolescents, "want to break the cycle of cultural insensitivity" (*From Age to Age*, no. 55). Now for the big words of caution: appearances may be deceptive! We must understand the cultural reality to which that adolescent returns every night—a very Latino home. Thus to get to that next level of dialogue with Hispanic youth, we must indeed know where they're coming from.

Hispanic Parent-Teen Relationships at Home

Many Latino youth are struggling with their cultural identity in addition to typical adolescent issues. Differences with their parents are apparent. The parents may speak only Spanish, but the young people's main language may be English. The parents may feel that there is something of their culture that is lost in their child: lack of interest in traditions, lack of respect for elders, listening to rap instead of Vicente (Fernández), poor skills in reading and writing Spanish. These differences are common to parent-child relationships in many cultures, but they are greatly compounded by the cultural struggles between traditional Latino values and the constant bombardment of mainstream American culture.

Differences in Life Experiences

It is very likely that the Hispanic youth you deal with have grown up with a different ideology and perspective on life than a suburban, Anglo child. It's likely that only one parent has the fortune of employment, that Mamá and Papá do not drive a new car, and that the kids have never been disciplined with a "time-out" but probably *have* had a good spanking on more than one occasion. In the inner city it is possible that tía and tío (aunt and uncle) live upstairs or in a different flat of the same building; that the child is being raised by a single parent, or perhaps the teen is even a single parent himself or herself; and that the young person may know someone who has been shot to death on his or her block.

Before this turns into a list of stereotypes, please understand that I realize that not every Hispanic youth comes from a grim or unpleasant situation, and that many have gone on to achieve their goals and lead wonderful lives. However, a lot of challenges remain in many communities. It sometimes takes more than a single generation to change habits and practices that have been engraved in a culture for hundreds of years . . .

or ones that are recent but even more harmful. No matter what the reality is, people who work in Hispanic youth ministry must avoid jumping to judgment and must listen to both youth and their parents in order to help them understand their differences and struggles. It is then that we will have the reward of seeing the faith move beyond Sunday worship and into the daily lives of Hispanic youth and their families.

Support of the Neighborhood Youth

The church serves as a gathering place for many Hispanics, whether it is for Sunday Mass or for social activities, bingo not excluded. In Chicago it is apparent how the church building itself serves as the neighborhood's focal point. Chicago churches of the early 1900s were built by ethnic communities in close proximity to one another as each new group of immigrants created its own social enclave. Many of these ethnic churches are now homes for new groups of immigrants, including Hispanics. Hispanics have a deep respect for the church (even the gang kids who always make the sign of the cross when passing in front of the building).

Therefore it is important that parishes, as a focal point for so many people's lives in the area, be committed to service of those in their presence. In inner-city parishes, location facilitates this involvement. But in suburbs and newer areas, the spread-out nature of urban planning makes this more difficult. Regardless of the physical situation, the parish's outreach to its community should never be compromised.

A key component of community outreach is good liturgy. Good liturgy says even more about what a parish stands for than a mission statement can portray. But paralleling good liturgy are the other forms of ministerial outreach in response to community needs. Before I talk about what makes liturgy attractive for Hispanic youth, let me share our parish's success in meeting community needs, because I believe that our success in liturgy is closely connected to our effective community outreach.

A Model of Commitment: Holy Cross/IHM Parish

I have had the good fortune to be part of a parish that is fully and actively committed to its neighborhood youth every day of the week, not just on Sundays. Holy Cross/IHM Parish is in the heart of a vibrant, densely populated Mexican neighborhood. Many residents are Spanish-speaking immigrants from Mexico or first-generation Mexican Americans; the average age is nineteen. With neighborhood issues such as immigration, poverty, drugs and alcoholism, and crime and gangs, it is easy to see the many challenges and opportunities for working with youth on a grassroots level.

Proactive Ministry

Holy Cross/IHM Parish works hard to be proactive in our approach to ministry in the community. We try to spark positive thinking and avoid the trap of working *reactively,* that is, only taking action when something happens that needs immediate attention: whether it be a recent pregnancy, argument, arrest, or act of violence. Granted, dropping everything and attending to these issues is a must, but unfortunately doing so can divert the focus away from proactive approaches to ministry, for example, starting an awareness program for pregnancy, or job training for gang members, or providing tutoring for high school dropouts. These preventative measures and programs, which affect youth in positive ways, increase your approachability. Positive word spreads.

"Going to School Today?" "No Way, Too Risky!"

A major concern in the neighborhood surrounding Holy Cross Church is that the closest public high school is over two miles away. This may not seem like troubling news, but to put it in perspective, that means kids will have to travel through more than *nine* different gang territories just to get to daily classes. Furthermore, for those kids who happen to have gang affiliation, that means they will be vulnerable—in enemy territory—essentially risking their lives every day. The common solution is to drop out of school; that is why the dropout rate in the neighborhood is atrocious (over 70 percent). Luckily kids who are "on the right track" have the good fortune to attend better schools that may be a greater distance away, and the parish supports them with scholarships and active participation in their school's leadership. But for at-risk youth who have a desire to better their lives through education, there is only a dead end. Literally.

In a breakthrough effort to serve the community, and with the support and funding of the Chicago Public Schools, Holy Cross/IHM Parish started the Sister Irene Dugan Institute in the spring of 1998. The Dugan Institute was created as an alternative high school geared toward at-risk youth, gang members, and former dropouts. The school runs year-round, including summers (when rival gang activity is at its greatest), and daily classes are from 3 p.m. to 9 p.m. Dugan Institute had an average attendance of twenty-five students during its first year. That means twenty-five kids were *not* hanging out on the corner, and instead were in a safe environment studying math and science—and liking it. The first year six graduates earned their high school diploma.

In a beautiful graduation ceremony inside Holy Cross Church, the graduates each expressed their gratitude to the parish for believing in them and offering them a second chance. One graduate summed up his speech, "And to all of you who didn't believe in us, we proved you wrong!" To me that was one of the greatest moments in the parish's history, and though it had not much to do with liturgy, it had everything to do with ministry and community. The next step of course was welcoming these youth into the presence of the larger parish community through the liturgy.

The Word Spreads; the Effect is Far Reaching

Concern for youth has sparked other parish programs and activities that may be targeted directly at groups other than youth but whose indirect result is better lives (physically and spiritually) for youth. The needs of parish communities may vary greatly—Dugan Alternative High School was started to address a specific need—but it is essential for the church to recognize and act on whatever needs exist. For some parishes the greatest need may be addressed through its efforts in liturgy; for others it may sway toward community service.

Community-service ideas that are within financial reach for a parish might include day-care programs, arts programs, after-school study hall or computer labs (look for corporate donations!), youth centers for safe sports and recreation, music opportunities (like mariachi classes), and parish partnerships with local businesses, public schools, park districts, the police, and city and state governments.

Vibrant Liturgy with Hispanic Youth

Okay, how do you take what you know about Hispanic youth culture and apply it to liturgical celebrations? Let me emphasize again that ministering with Hispanic people is a big step toward understanding Hispanic culture, and understanding Hispanic culture is critical to celebrating liturgy with Hispanic people. Drawing on my own experience, I'd like to highlight three important elements that make liturgy vibrant for Hispanic people.

Celebrate Cultural Events

Particular customs in Hispanic culture are a vital part of their liturgical celebrations. There are traditions such as a *quinceañera* (the celebration of a girl's fifteenth birthday) and the presentation of certain symbols and gifts at weddings. There are street processions: Las Posadas (Mary and Joseph's searching for room at the inn) during Christmas and El Viacrucis (the way of the cross) on Good Friday. Hispanic people's deep devotion is celebrated with festive Marian celebrations, such as the feast of Our Lady of Guadalupe. The mode of celebrating these events often includes mariachi ensembles and folkloric dances. Taken together, these deep devotional practices are an inherent part of being a Hispanic Catholic.

Especially for those not familiar with Hispanic customs, it is important to avoid thinking of them as quaint customs or liturgical aberrations. Rather, they are traditions that stem from popular religiosity and are treasured by a culture that has celebrated them for generations. It is also important to understand that within these customs are variances particular to different Latin American cultures. For example, Puerto Ricans may celebrate a certain feast differently than Guatemalans would. A song sung to Mary in Mexico would be done differently by Cubans. And variances in food . . . well, that's sufficient cause for another article (on recipes).

It is impossible within the scope of this article to adequately explain the origin and proper observance of these cultural celebrations. *Primero Dios: Hispanic Liturgical Resource,* by Mark Francis and Arturo Pérez (Chicago: Liturgy Training Publications, 1997) and *Misa, Mesa y Musa: Liturgy in the U.S. Hispanic Church,* compiled and edited by Ken Davis, OFM Conv (Schiller Park, IL: World Liturgy Publications, 1997) are helpful resources for those who are unfamiliar with them. Of course nothing substitutes for learning the customs from Hispanic people themselves.

Hospitality and Inclusion

Hospitality and inclusion are important values for Hispanic people, which carries over into Hispanic liturgies. When a parish is active in the community, it earns status as God's house where all are welcome. Having earned that status, the parish must bring the community together through its liturgies. All contribute themselves through prayer and participation, for "it is the same Lord . . . who gathers all generations. . . . Many gifts, but the same Spirit" (*From Age to Age,* no. 8). In this regard it is impossible to imagine a stranger joining the worshiping community without being welcomed and greeted.

To further emphasize belonging and welcome, the worship aids used can say a lot about a church's commitment to Hispanics and youth. World Library Publication's bilingual *Celebremos/Let Us Celebrate* missal is an example of an inclusive resource for liturgy with Hispanic youth, especially in Spanish-speaking or bilingual communities. This type of resource is an excellent means for guiding someone through the liturgy, and it gives all readings and Mass texts side by side in English and Spanish. For families in which the different generations speak different languages, it allows them to worship together, making all feel welcome. In choosing or designing your worship aids, be sure that they reflect this inclusiveness.

Indeed a great accomplishment for a parish is to have its youth participating in Mass—both as members of the assembly and through ministry roles. Inviting them to participate shows that the parish needs and values their involvement. In order to get youth into active liturgical roles, sometimes you have to start "outside" the liturgy to attract them, and then use that attraction to involve them later. For example, many Hispanic parishes have a Good Friday stations of the cross procession through the streets of their neighborhood. One means of outreach is to ask various youth who normally do not attend Mass to take turns carrying the cross between stations, or they can help build an *altarcito* (a small decorated table) for one of the stations. That simple action can give them a sense of belonging and active contribution to the parish community. Later ask those same youth to help usher at the Sunday Mass, and they will probably agree to it because of the experience they had earlier.

Hispanic youth typically have a deep sense of reverence for the church and the liturgy. Yet this reverence may be coupled with a sense of "Mass is only for me to watch, not do." This misunderstanding can prevent people from getting involved, even if they have the desire to. Youth who may be intimidated by more "visible" roles are usually open to simpler means of involvement, such as the presentation of the gifts. Before Mass begins, approach and personally invite various young people in the congregation (even newcomers to your parish) to be responsible for presenting the offerings. It is a great way to extend a welcome and perhaps an invitation to other ministries down the road.

In bilingual communities youth are many times the ideal (and sometimes only) persons to proclaim the word effectively in Spanish and in

English. You can take a "we need you" approach, and if cautiously applied, that encouragement might be enough to persuade talented youth to take on certain roles in the liturgy that they might not have initiated otherwise.

Hispanic Liturgical Music

For all young people, but especially for Hispanic young people, music can provide the initial attraction to participating in liturgical celebrations. Music can move our hearts and serve as a vehicle for prayer—communal and personal. Youth long to have their hearts moved through prayer, and when they experience it, prayer brings fulfillment. For this reason I will spend more time discussing the third element for vibrant worship with Hispanics: liturgical music.

Hispanic culture is rich in all styles of liturgical music, from classical to popular. It has roots in a variety of styles: Caribbean, *norteña* (coming from the northern part of Mexico), mariachi, folk, traditional, European, contemporary, and so on. These styles have pretty much paralleled that of the English repertoire—that is, just as there is English hymnody, folk, or contemporary music, there is Hispanic hymnody, folk, or contemporary music. (When using the term *Spanish,* know that it generally refers to anything coming from Spain; *Hispanic* is the more appropriate term for Spanish-language music used throughout the United States and Latin America.)

Contemporary Music in Spanish

Modern composers are creating some wonderful music completely in Spanish. These new pieces are rooted in time-honored tradition and may be some of the youth's favorite songs. Contemporary music today ranges in style from slower, more meditative songs to new, up-tempo songs for mariachi. Caribbean-style percussion or Latin guitar rhythms such as *huapango, ranchero,* and *bolero* make for driving beats that bring life to new tunes and texts. Young people embrace this music because it brings "freshness and variety to our current musical genres and . . . infuse[s] sacred music with energy and vitality" (*From Age to Age,* no. 64).

Newer pieces have also served to update the traditional repertoire of the Hispanic church. For example, many songs to Our Lady of Guadalupe stem from a pre–Vatican Council II tradition of deep personal devotion and even adoration of the Virgin, and therefore do not reflect newer perspectives on theology, community, and liturgy. Contemporary Marian tunes and texts have enhanced the Hispanic repertoire with music that is assembly friendly and that reflects post–Vatican Council II views of Mary as the first disciple and the mother of God. Many of these songs also reflect a powerful theme in Hispanic music: calling on God's help in the fight for social justice.

Bilingual Music

The area of uncharted waters in liturgical music today is bilingualism: the mixing of Spanish and English within a single song. As the church in the United States moves toward more multicultural liturgies, the issue of bilingual (and multilingual) music arises. Composers such as Pedro Rubalcava, Jaime Cortéz, Bob Hurd, Eleazar Cortés, Lorenzo Florián, and Donna Peña have contributed substantially to this repertoire. For parishes that have an integrated community, bilingual music tends to be a perfect solution— singing in both languages, mixing and matching, just as everyday conversation might switch back and forth. Other parishes may have separate English-speaking and Spanish-speaking communities that need to come together for special occasions. In either case bilingual music can help bridge the language gap. Hispanic youth take to this music very well because they are more likely to be bilingual than their parents and are less resistant to musical and textual change.

The refrain of a typical bilingual song might include a phrase or two in Spanish followed by a phrase or two in English. More recently greater care has been taken by publishers to include complete refrains in Spanish and English, allowing communities to switch languages or use both as necessary. And composers have incorporated creative solutions into their text setting, such as having an assembly sing a refrain in one language while the choir sings a descant or harmony in another, or making use of short phrases that either Spanish- or English-speaking people can easily learn, while leaving more complicated texts to be sung by cantors. Taizé-style pieces that use common Latin or Greek texts for the refrain and alternating Spanish and English verses are also growing in popularity.

Don't Forget Traditional Music

A common stereotype is that all youth music has to be fast and upbeat. Hispanic music is particularly known for its driving rhythms and danceable styles. But my experience is that youth want to have their reflective moments, too. A youth Mass in which everything is fast and yippee-skippy is like having too much caffeine and being stuck in fast-forward. Youth need to be offered the experience of liturgy as prayer, which should include joy and celebration as well as solemn, reflective moments. "We have a responsibility to invite youth to appreciate a variety of traditional and contemporary liturgical music styles" (*From Age to Age,* no. 66). Furthermore, recall that just as the Sacramentary contains the rubrics for Masses "with children," not "for children," our Masses for younger generations must be celebrations "with youth" and not "for youth." In fact, "a weekly *youth-only* Mass can discourage youth from experiencing the prayer of the whole church and can isolate teens from their families" and the greater community (*From Age to Age,* no. 93). A variety of traditional and contemporary music helps the entire community to worship together.

I mentioned earlier that many Hispanic parents feel that Hispanic traditions are becoming lost as youth become more and more integrated into popular American culture. This concern extends to musical tradition also. Many of the youth in our parishes may not know the songs that their parents knew by heart. But this break between generations does not need to happen. Do not underestimate the intelligence and curiosity of youth; traditional styles of music may be attractive to many young people. Why? Because for them it is new. And for youth, new is good. A chant-style song could be a great hit with your group, and they might not even realize that it is from the twelfth century! You may even find that sacred Latin chants (such as *Pange Lingua, Adoro te Devote,* and *Regina Caeli*) bridge the language gap better than newer bilingual songs.

Finally, know that a valuable repertoire from Spain is part of the standard repertoire of Hispanic music today. The repertoire comes from composers such as Cesáreo Gabaráin, Francisco Palazón, Juan Espinosa, and Carmelo Erdozáin. This music is generally very good, with texts based on the Scriptures and melodies that have worked well in all Latin American cultures. Other substantial contributors to the Hispanic repertoire include Lucien Deiss, Carlos Rosas, and Mary Frances Reza. This music is "tried and true" for a reason, and it will work with any generation.

Your Turn Now

Attracting youth—Hispanic or otherwise—to active participation in liturgy is a constant challenge for anyone. My best advice is to be creative. Through Hispanic ministry, take the plunge into Hispanic culture—learn the music, enjoy the food, and then let the liturgy reflect your life together as a faith community. Use music to invite Hispanic youth to be part of parish ministry, because music offers a little something for everyone and is thus the best possible welcome to your youth. Lastly, always love the youth. They are not the future—they are the *now*.

Youth and Liturgy:
An African American Perspective

Valerie Shields

Valerie Shields teaches religious studies at Holy Cross High School in New Orleans. She is also the founder of the youth ministry program at Xavier University's Institute for Black Catholic Studies.

Take a moment and ask yourself what images come to mind when you hear "Black church." Do you see a scene from a Blues Brothers movie with spirited preaching, an enthusiastic gospel choir, and dancing in the aisles? Do you have a hard time reconciling this image with formal Roman Catholic liturgy? Well, I'm here to tell you that the two can become one in a way that does justice to both.

However, you cannot just make spirited worship happen by getting the choir to sing a few gospel songs and your priests to develop rhythm and cadence in their delivery. Spirited worship flows from the heart of a people that know they are loved by God and freed by God's grace. The spirited worship that characterizes African American liturgy flows from our cultural experience of knowing God's grace amid slavery and oppression. In this article I will name some of the elements that characterize the spirited worship of African American Catholics.

Unfortunately many African American young people are cut off from their historical roots. We must help them recover their rich cultural heritage, which will root their spirituality. Appropriate liturgical worship guides them to appreciate and embrace the richness and wonder of their Black identity, reinforcing the knowledge of who they are: "a chosen race, a royal priesthood, a holy nation, God's own people" (1 Pet. 2:9). This is an important goal to keep in mind when planning liturgies in which African American youth are present.

Even if your congregation does not include any African American youth, infusing your liturgy with African American music and themes can enrich your community's worship. African Americans bring the church the gift of being enthusiastic and moving in their praise of God! Celebrating cultural experiences and traditions in your worship is an important reminder that we are a diverse church, rich in our diversity and in our unity.

Elements of Authentic African American Liturgical Experience

Perhaps the central point about the spirit that characterizes African American worship is that it is at once both formal and informal. That is, it contains ordered elements, but there is also room for individual freedom of expression. This informal freedom might be expressed in spontaneous praise, in liturgical movement, or through music. For the most part, the typical Roman Catholic parish liturgy lacks that informal and spontaneous expression.

This free and informal aspect of worship is not something you can program in a community unaccustomed to that style. However, some key elements that characterize vibrant African American liturgies you can plan for: stirring music, moving drama and ritual, poignant themes, a rich environment, and of course, inclusiveness. I will comment on each of these and also give some examples for your consideration.

At the end of the article (page 157), I have included an appendix with a liturgy outline for a eucharistic celebration of Black History Month. The outline offers a good example of the application of the elements that characterize vibrant African American liturgy.

Stirring Music

For African Americans good liturgy must have music that is upbeat, soul stirring, and reverent. Music gives hope, it sustains, it heals, and helps one to "get over." We are a singing people! We have a song even when we may have little else. In fact some people think we sing at the strangest and even inappropriate times.

Music is an intrinsic part of the African American community. It is as much a carrier of our history and faith as the spoken or written word. Ours is a diverse music—both African and American, simple and profound, traditional and contemporary. The sounds of both Christian rap and contemporary gospel may punctuate our worship services. At the same time we must teach appreciation for the Negro spirituals and soul gospel music that have been at the heart of African American spirituality for the last two centuries. It is impossible to conceive of the African American religious tradition in any authentic sense without these songs of surviva , liberation, hope, and celebration. A good source for this treasury of music is *Lead Me, Guide Me: The African American Hymnal* (Chicago: GIA Publications, 1987).

Musical instruments are a key part of African American youth liturgies. One vital instrument is the drum. Sometimes drums are called the heartbeat of Africa. Commonly used to call worshipers together to prepare themselves for the service, the drum is also a symbol by which the community is called to follow the beat of the drummer, Jesus, the Lord.

Moving Drama and Ritual

Not only are we a singing people, but we are also a very demonstrative people. We revel in our pomp and circumstance. We march, dance, wave, shout, nod, and genuflect. We make a joyful noise unto the Lord. Liturgy for African Americans is not what we do; it is who we are. If there is any word that most accurately describes worship in the African American church, it is *authenticity*. We stumble only when we try to be other than ourselves.

It is important that liturgy, as ritual, celebrates our sense of being community and affirms our feelings of togetherness. This is sometimes emphasized through physical contact, such as joining hands or touching in some way, so that spiritual togetherness is reaffirmed and heightened by a ritual form of physical togetherness. The emphasis is on community rather than on the individual, on fellowship rather than uniqueness. It is also important for African Americans to experience spiritual involvement—which includes emotional involvement—as part of liturgy. The worship service is expected to be emotionally and spiritually involving. When these things occur, African Americans are apt to say, "We had church today!"

The liturgy of the word is one of the primary ritual activities in African American worship. Preachers are and always have been the bulwark of the African American community because of their ability to read, interpret, and deliver the meaning of God's word in a way that youth can apply to their daily life. Preachers take poetic license with the Scriptures, painting moving images of biblical events and delivering inspired messages. Their rhythmic and repetitive cadence totally engages listeners, so that they leave the service with determination to enact what has been learned.

Good African American poetry, mime, ballet, modern dance, choral reading, and African movements can be artistically and meaningfully incorporated into youth liturgies. These expressions take time, and African American liturgies are often longer than liturgies of other cultural backgrounds. In mainstream U.S. culture, time is not to be wasted but rather cautiously guarded and sparingly meted out. But for African Americans, time is for precious living, joyful celebrating, and meaningful encountering. Hence good liturgy is not measured by how many minutes it takes but only by the energy and movement of the Spirit.

African American rituals have a way of going back to the past and bringing it to the present. Water, earth (soil), large black pots, trees, plants, incense, branches, African brooms, patchwork quilts, and cow bells are a few symbols that are used to connect African American historical origins to the present. For example we sometimes incorporate a libations ceremony in which water is poured in the direction of the four winds: north, south, east, and west. The cup is then passed to individuals representing our African past and American present.

Soil is used as a reminder that our fathers and mothers came here, lived, loved, struggled, and built their lives. At this place their love and labor rose like the sun and gave strength and meaning to the day. For them who gave so much, we give in return. On this same soil, we will sow our seeds and build and move in unity and strength.

The black iron pot can be incorporated in any Black culture liturgical celebration. It is symbolic of God's presence in our midst. Former slaves claimed that an iron pot turned upside down was a sign that God was with them. Trees, plants, and branches are other symbols that could be used in Black culture liturgical celebrations as symbols of life. A good source for further reading is *African American Christian Worship,* by Melva Wilson Costen (Nashville: Abingdon Press).

Quilts are often used in Black History Month observances because they are symbolic of the importance of the oral tradition in African American culture. Quilt patterns and stitches had codes that could be read by slaves as they traveled along the Underground Railroad. A good source for further reading is *Hidden in Plain View: A Secret Story of Quilts and the Underground Railroad,* by Jacqueline L. Tobin and Raymond G. Dobard, PhD (New York: Doubleday).

The broomstick is a symbol of matrimony. In many African American wedding ceremonies today, couples are reclaiming the tradition of "jumping the broom." They have elected to embrace the customs of our ancestors and witness to the faith of their forebears. The broomstick ritual was occasionally added to the regular wedding ceremony at the request of slaves who felt that this act authenticated the regular rite. For further reading see *African American Christian Worship.*

God does belong to all ages, and rituals used in African American youth worship should reflect how we can find God in our lived experience. Ritual must speak to the needs of African American youth, reflecting their problems, affirming their worth in God's sight, and inspiring them to seek sound moral solutions to daily choices. Rites, ceremonies, and liturgies, like theology, cannot be developed in isolation from the crucial problems we experience. On the contrary, ritual should affirm the liberating presence of God in our lived human experience.

Poignant Themes

In our liturgical celebrations we continually offer our complete selves to God, including all our joys and struggles. For young people this includes the struggle to make sense of life. In particular for African American youth this includes the legacy of slavery and discrimination. As a result of this legacy many of them live in difficult situations in which hope is a scarce commodity. Hence African American worship often reflects the poignant theme of a captive and alienated people in a strange land, a people in pursuit of liberation, freedom, health, and wholeness.

Connected with this central theme, African Americans also celebrate virginity; rites of passage, loss, transformation; the seven principles, or Nguzo Saba; Black History Month; the Black saints; and our African American heroes and heroines, both past and contemporary. (See the appendix to this article for a calendar of Black Catholic celebrations.) African Americans also remember imprisoned friends and relatives, people with AIDS, homeless people, and people killed or maimed from community violence. The lectionary provides many opportunities for developing these themes for those who are attentive to them.

Rich Environment

> The *Constitution on the Sacred Liturgy* teaches that worship and art are linked together intimately, and that the Church, which is the universal People of God, admits of no single style of art in worship. . . .
>
> African-American traditions of art arising from the genius and gifts of the Black people are a part of that "treasury of art" that must enhance and express what is signified in the liturgy: the worship of God and the building up of God's people. (NCCB, *In Spirit and Truth*, p. 6)

Color and pageantry characterize African American worship. Every sense must be stimulated. The bright colors of African culture are pleasing to the sight and inviting to the spirit. For example, we often use Kente cloth, with its historical connection to African culture, to drape the altar, lecterns, walls, or other places in the worship area. Live and colorful plants, fruits, and vegetables are often used to help create the liturgical environment. Not only are they beautiful and fragrant, but they are fruits of Mother Earth, which reminds us of Mother God.

Incense is used frequently in African American worship. Historically Africans have used incense in a variety of ways. Incense and its smoke symbolize the cleansing of the sacred space, purging it of all evils and satanic spirits and driving away dissension within the community.

A unique element of African American worship is the use of the African American flag. The motto of the flag is "Persevering Through Time." The flag's colors are red, white, blue, black, green, purple, and gold. Purple symbolizes the regal history of African Americans. Gold symbolizes the riches of Africa. The red, white, and blue stripes symbolize the integral part African Americans play, have played, and will play in America's greatness. The eight-pointed black stars symbolize each individual African American. The stars' theme is "Black Stars Can Shine Too." The African American flag can be carried in procession and appropriately displayed in the church sanctuary.

The African American flag is a strong and positive symbol in the African American community. It is not a political or racist flag; rather it represents the progress African Americans have made in overcoming adversity. People of all colors can embrace its symbols of hope and pride. (The African American flag can be ordered from Daton, Inc., 1-800-32-FLAGS).

Inclusiveness

Because African Americans as a people have often experienced the pain of exclusion, inclusiveness has become an important value for us. In regard to worship, I encourage you to think about inclusiveness in two ways. The first way is by helping young people feel welcome at the liturgy. Much has already been said about this in the other articles in this book. African American youth respond to many of the same things as young people of other cultures. They respond to music, preaching, and rituals that are alive and inspired. They respond to worship that speaks to the reality of their daily lives. They respond to personal invitations to share their gifts. They respond to mentors who nurture their gifts and participation. The more of these elements you include in your planning, the more young people will feel included.

Another way to think about inclusiveness is in your use of all the elements already discussed in this article. If you make an effort to include those elements, you will find youth responding positively to your liturgies regardless of their cultural background.

Some Final Remarks

Meaningful change requires education. The Book of Proverbs teaches, "Train children in the right way, and when old, they will not stray" (Prov. 22:6). In this article I have provided some basic information for understanding what constitutes vibrant worship with and for youth from an African American perspective.

But what I have shared with you does not in any way cover all that could and should be considered. I strongly urge you to continue your training by reading and reflecting on the NCCB document *Plenty Good Room: The Spirit and Truth of African American Worship*. In the words of Rev. Donald M. Clark:

> No one who really cares about adapting Catholic worship to make it truly Black and authentically Catholic should make another move before reading this document. It is no detailed "how to do" publication . . . *Plenty Good Room* is, rather, a reflection on solid principles, interesting facts, and necessary information that ought to be the foundations of efforts at transforming liturgy for African American Catholic people. (From the back cover)

Keep in mind that while the elements I have described apply most fully to African American liturgical experience, they can also be adapted and applied to liturgies in which several different cultures are represented in the assembly. They may even be used in liturgies without any African American people present. This is the blessing and grace of our multicultural church—that we can all grow richer from one another's gifts.

Appendix A: We Must Not Forget: A Liturgy Outline for Black History Month

Background

Remember the famous quote by George Santayana: "Those who cannot remember the past are condemned to repeat it." Black History Month celebrations are held in February in the United States with that purpose in mind. They help people of African descent keep their past and their present history in a healthy balance, and they help people of all cultures recognize the cultural contributions of African Americans.

Throughout the Bible God continually calls people to recall the events that symbolize God's saving power in their history. The feasts that were established in Israel helped the people remember and celebrate their past. For the same reasons, given the centrality of Christian faith in the history and lives of African Americans, it is important to remember and celebrate as a church the spiritual contributions of African Americans. The liturgy outlined in this appendix can be used by any church to celebrate Black History Month. In looking over this outline you also may find liturgical elements that can be incorporated into other multicultural liturgies.

I want to be clear that the celebration of Black History Month does not have to be confined to a single liturgical celebration. Communities can focus on a different element of African American spirituality on each Sunday of the month of February. For example the first Sunday in February could be a celebration of the African American church, highlighting its style of worship, the role of the Black clergy, and the various functions the Black church has played in the history of Black people.

The second Sunday could focus on Black music. Examples of the different forms of Black church music, the Negro spirituals, gospel, metered hymns, and congregational singing—just to name a few—could be presented. Black music should be considered not just as an art form but as a "survival form."

The third Sunday could be used to look at the Black family experience. This could be an intergenerational experience with grandparents, great-grandparents, newly married individuals, single parents, fathers, and mothers called on to share their experiences. It would be interesting to have children and youth speak about the joys, problems, stresses, and satisfactions of family life.

The fourth Sunday could explore the importance of community involvement. African Americans do not separate the sacred and the secular. Thus we must be involved in our community to be the church in the world.

Preparation

Suggestions for the Liturgical Environment

In preparing your worship space, be attentive to creating an environment that is rich to all the senses. Consider incorporating the following elements:
1. Red, black, and green are the colors for a Black history celebration. Red stands for love, living blood, emotion, ardor, strife, anger, passion, and warmth. Green symbolizes life, love, freshness, growth, perspective, and visibility. Black symbolizes solidarity, strength, power, infinity, freshness, healing, peace, visibility, growth, and the divine. Use these colors on banners, wall coverings, and worship aids.
2. If you can find one, use a big, black iron pot as part of your liturgical decor. African slaves made noise with such pots when the community gathered in secrecy, to drown out their singing so that their slave masters would not know where they were gathered.
3. Use lots of green plants, both large and small.
4. Carry the African American flag in the procession, and then display it where it will be a visible—but not primary—focus.
5. In your gathering area or commons, display pictures of various African Americans who have made contributions to Black history.

Suggestions for Music

For the liturgy use Negro spirituals, metered hymns, or appropriate gospel and contemporary songs. The following freedom songs can be found in *Lead Me, Guide Me: The African American Catholic Hymnal* (GIA Publications, 1987):

- "Amazing Grace"
- "Swing Low, Sweet Chariot"
- "Steal Away to Jesus"
- "Come by Here"
- "Come Out the Wilderness"
- "Deep River"
- "Free at Last"
- "Glory, Glory, Hallelujah"

Liturgical Ministers

Involve as many youth as possible in the various liturgical ministries. Youth can be trained as ministers of hospitality (ushers), eucharistic ministers, lectors, altar servers, ministers of music, and sacred dancers.

All the liturgical ministers except those of hospitality and music should be part of the entrance procession. All ministers should wear some kind of attire or symbol that reflects and identifies their particular ministry. This helps create the ritual drama that is so important in African American worship.

Because the liturgy is a drama, all who will participate need to rehearse their roles. Each person should be taught not just the mechanics of her or his ministry but also the ministry's liturgical and spiritual meaning.

Liturgy Outline

The following outline contains suggestions for movement, commentary, and music for a Roman Catholic eucharistic celebration. Only those parts of the Mass for which I have specific suggestions are listed. Adapt these to your congregation and situation.

Gathering Rite

Preparation of the Sacred Space

As the people assemble, a musician begins to softly play melodies of freedom or spiritual songs. When the assembly has gathered and remains sitting, sacred dancers bless the worship space with incense and sacred movement. The dancers come from the four corners of the worship space. They should encircle the entire worship space in movement and come together in the center to spread incense around the sacred space. Then a welcome dance begins to the beat of drums. The dancers proceed in formation to meet the entrance procession. Before the entrance procession begins, a youth commentator welcomes the congregation in these or similar words:

> Good morning, my name is _____. On behalf of [name of church], I welcome you to our eucharistic celebration as we celebrate Black History Month.
>
> Carter G. Woodson, the originator of Black History Month, knew the importance of knowing one's self and one's history. The knowledge of our history roots us deeply. We are a creative, ingenious, surviving, God-centered people. Let us honor the

persons and recall the events of African American history. We recognize the historical heritage of [name of city] and of [church or school name]. We pray that God will help us to learn about the past and from the past, so as to live today with higher self-esteem and greater self-awareness.

As we begin today's celebration, let us take a moment to recall our history. Millions have gone before us, teaching, producing, sharing, and caring. Many of our ancestors died during the terrible Middle Passage from Africa to the Americas and now rest in the Atlantic Ocean.

Our ancestors who survived that dangerous passage arrived on these shores, and with a God that helped them to make a way out of no way, withstood the cruelties and rigors of slavery. They were creative and wise. They took a remnant of their African culture and merged it with what they gleaned from Western culture, and this indigenous Black culture flourished on American soil.

We salute the historic efforts of those dedicated to the liberation of all people. We take our hats off to abolitionists and freedom fighters throughout history. We salute ourselves during this [number] annual Black History Month. May there come a time when all society celebrates Black history. Again, welcome! Please stand and join in singing our Black national anthem, "Lift Every Voice and Sing."

After singing the anthem, the procession begins.

Entrance Song: "Come Out of the Wilderness"

Greeting and Opening Prayer

Let us pray: O God of life and history, who acted in the beginning and acts today, we praise your eternal mercy and justice that sustains us in our strength and frailty.

We thank you for the lives of slaves, who praised your name despite the tyranny that oppressed them. We thank you for those who always protested injustice and rallied for change and transformation in the home, church, and society. Give us your strength to follow them as your instruments of change and transformation. We ask this through our Lord and Savior Jesus Christ, your beloved Son, who lives and reigns with you in the unity of the Holy Spirit. Amen.

Liturgy of the Word

The Scripture readings for this celebration are taken from the lectionary options for the votive Mass of the Triumph of the Holy Cross.

First Reading: Exod. 12:1–8,11–14

Responsorial Psalm: Ps. 68:31–35

An appropriate song may be played here, or a song response could be sung between the spoken verses.

Second Reading: Heb. 5:7–9

Gospel Acclamation: "Hallelujah, Salvation and Glory"

During the Gospel acclamation the sacred dancers lead the presider in procession to the ambo. They incense the book of the Gospels and the presider. After the choir finishes singing, the drums are played softly while the presider proclaims the Gospel. After the proclamation the drums build in volume to a loud climax and stop.

Gospel: Mark 8:31–34

Homily

The choir may sing an appropriate song before the homily is given.

Profession of Faith

> *Presider:* Do you believe in God, the almighty Father and master of our destiny, who guides all creation by his spirit?
>
> *Assembly:* Yes, I do believe!
>
> *Presider:* Do you believe in Jesus Christ, God's Son, conceived by the Spirit, anointed by him at his baptism, who was crucified, died, was buried, rose, and is now seated at the right hand of the Father to fill all creation with his blessings?
>
> *Assembly:* Yes, I do believe!
>
> *Presider:* Do you believe in the Holy Spirit, the Lord and Giver of Life, who came to the Apostles and the whole church at Pentecost, and who has come to us in Baptism and Confirmation?
>
> *Assembly:* Yes, I do believe!
>
> *Presider:* Do you believe in the Spirit's power to make us the one, holy Catholic church, the true Body of Christ, through the forgiveness

of sins, the resurrection of the body, and the promise of life everlasting?

Assembly: Yes, I do believe!

Prayer of the Faithful

Lector: As a community of faith, how important it is for us to remember our history. As we look at the events of our past we must never forget those individuals, Black and white, who sacrificed so that we could enjoy the freedoms that exist in America today. Please respond, "Lord, let us not forget."

1. For the greatness of your creation that shaped the lives and community stories of our ancestors, our families, and ourselves. Let us pray to the Lord . . .
2. For the opportunity to celebrate the magnificent contributions of African Americans past and present, we pray . . .
3. For those inspired women and men who have taught us our own history, we pray . . .
4. On this day we remember Carter G. Woodson, historian, architect, and chief celebrant of Black History Month, and Maulana Karenga, writer and driving force behind Kwanzaa. For all who remind us to learn our heritage and to uphold the community values that are a part of that heritage, we pray . . .
5. That we may become a nation whose pride is found in its loving care of all the forgotten people of our society, we pray . . .
6. That all youth may learn and hold on to lessons of past generations in the spirit of Sankofa, we pray . . .
7. That the church may always give clear witness to its belief that God is the absolute measure of all we do, we pray . . .

Presider: O Redeemer, we thank you for life, health, and strength. We thank you for the world, for ideas, for creativity, for family, for ourselves, for today. Lord, help us to live today, this day, a special and extraordinary day in an ordinary way. Help us to live this day so well that when the history of this day is written, we can hear God say about today: "Well done, my good and faithful servant!" We ask this through Christ our Lord. Amen.

Liturgy of the Eucharist

There are many fine musical arrangements to choose from for the eucharistic liturgy. Choose one that allows as much congregational singing as possible.

Preparation of the Gifts

It is recommended that the congregation's gifts (financial, food, clothing, and so on) be brought to the altar in the offertory procession before the bread, water, and wine is brought forward. The sacred dancers lead the offertory procession to the sound of the drums. A dancer could be placed in between each gift that is being brought forth. As the presider receives each gift, he raises the offering in prayer and thanksgiving to God.

Eucharistic Prayer

The fourth eucharistic prayer is recommended because of its emphasis on salvation, freedom, and joy.

Communion Song: "He Will Remember Me"

Communion Meditation

For the Communion meditation, someone could read a poem or short reflection. Or the choir could sing a special meditation song. The sacred dancers may also provide reflective movement during this time.

Concluding Rites

Final Blessing

Presider: As disciples of Jesus, servants of the Gospel, and neighbors to all, go in peace to love and serve the Lord.
All: Thanks be to God.

Before the recessional song, the entire congregation could join hands and sing "We Shall Overcome."

Recessional Song: "Everything Is a Day of Thanksgiving"

Appendix B:
Calendar of Catholic Black History Celebrations

January: Martin Luther King Jr.'s Birthday Observance

Since Dr. King's death over thirty years ago, a generation has been born that never knew him in the flesh. We must not make the awful mistake of assuming everybody remembers him. A brief biographical review should be given at all services recognizing Dr. King. Youth should be included on the program, and older adults should recall the benefits that resulted from Dr. King's life and death. George Santayana was correct when he said, "Those who cannot remember the past are condemned to repeat it." We must repeat over and over again the legacy Dr. King left, and we must stride toward making justice a reality.

February: Black History Month Observance

> This day shall be a day of remembrance for you. You shall celebrate it as a festival to the Lord. . . . You shall observe the festival of unleavened bread, for on this very day I brought your companies out of the land of Egypt: you shall observe this day throughout your generations as a perpetual ordinance. (Exod. 12:14,17)

Carter G. Woodson recognized the importance of knowing one's history. He began the celebration of Black history. Today many Black Catholic churches celebrate Black History Month. We have a past, a present, and a future in Christ Jesus. Millions have gone before us. The knowledge of our history roots us deeply, with the legacy of a creative, ingenious, surviving, God-centered people. Our history shows us possibilities and builds community.

February: National Day of Prayer for the African American Family

The National Day of Prayer for the African American Family was founded in 1989 during a gathering of Black Catholics in the Archdiocese of Atlanta. At this gathering those in Black leadership were sharing the problems, pain, and dreams of the Black community. Fr. James E. Goode, OFM, addressed the assembly on the power of prayer and called the nation to pray on the first Sunday of Black History Month. He then named it the National Day of Prayer for the African American Family. This day is set aside for us to give special thanks to God for our families and to place our every care in the arms of Jesus. How to celebrate the day:

- Worship and pray as a family for all African American families.
- Celebrate a meal together and tell your family's story.
- Make a family resolution, no matter how big or small. Strive to fulfill that resolution during the year.

The following prayer is to be read during the National Day of Prayer for the African American Family:

> God of mercy and God of love, we place our African American families before you today. May we be proud of our history and never forget those who paid a great price for our liberation. Bless us one by one, and keep our hearts and minds fixed on higher ground. Help us to live for you and not for ourselves, and may we cherish and proclaim the gift of life. Bless our parents, guardians, grandparents, children, relatives, and friends. Give us the amazing grace to be the salt of the earth and the light of the world. Help us as your children to live in such a way that the beauty and greatness of authentic love is reflected in all that we say and do. Anoint with healing those who are less fortunate, especially the motherless, the fatherless, the homeless, the broken, the sick, and the lonely. Bless our departed family members and friends. May they be led into the light of your dwelling place and gaze upon you forever. Then Lord, when this earthly journey is ended, give us a resting place where we will never grow old, where we will share the fullness of redemption and shout the victory for all eternity. This we ask in the precious name of Jesus, our Savior and blessed assurance. Amen. Holy Mother of God, pray for us.

November: Black Catholic History Month

The first celebration of Black Catholic History Month was held in November 1990 in various U.S. cities with the celebration of Saint Martin de Porres's feast day. On 3 November of that year, a liturgy celebrated the 350th anniversary of Saint Martin's transition into eternal life. November is also a time to celebrate Black people's contributions to the Roman Catholic tradition.

December 26–January 1: Kwanzaa Celebrations

Kwanzaa is a Swahili word for "firstfruits." It is an African American celebration founded by Dr. Maulana Ron Karenga as an opportunity to teach and pass on aspects of African American culture. Stories are told, reminding participants of the historical struggles and challenges of African Americans. Prayer and praise are also important elements of the Kwanzaa celebration. Seven principles, the Nguzo Saba, are the focus of Kwanzaa. Therefore, Kwanzaa is a cultural, religious, and political celebration within the Black Catholic church. It is cultural in that African Americans come together to celebrate heritage, genius, and destiny. It is religious because it provides an opportunity for prayer and praise to a God who can make a way out of no way. It is political because it reminds us of the work that is yet to be done in the area of social justice and empowerment.

Kwanzaa is usually celebrated for seven days beginning December 26 and culminating with a feast on January 1. Although Kwanzaa is celebrated during the Christmas season, it should not be confused as a substitute or alternative for Christmas. Instead it is a distinct celebration full of symbolism, action, songs, and storytelling. Kwanzaa reminds us that we have much to celebrate despite the winters of our lives. As a people of faith, it is a time to give thanks for the life-giving signs around us that feed and nourish our spirit.

Here are the seven principles of Kwanzaa:
1. *umoja*—unity
2. *kujichagulia*—self-determination
3. *ujima*—collective work and responsibility
4. *ujamaa*—familyhood and cooperative economics
5. *nia*—purpose
6. *kuumba*—creativity
7. *imani*—faith

The seven symbols of Kwanzaa are:
1. *mkeka*—a place mat of straw, which is a traditional African item
2. *kinara*—a candle holder for seven candles
3. *mishumaa saba*—the seven candles of red, black, and green
4. *mazao*—a variety of fruit
5. *vibunzi*—ears of corn representing the number of children in the home
6. *zawadi*—gifts for children (should be something educational)
7. *kikombe cha umoja*—unity or community cup

The Black liberation flag (red, black, and green) is displayed during Kwanzaa celebrations to remind the community of its mission to liberate Black people throughout the world.

Liturgical Catechesis:
A Parish Workshop Model

Lisa-Marie Calderone-Stewart

Lisa-Marie Calderone-Stewart is the associate director of early adolescent ministry for the Archdiocese of Milwaukee and was the chairperson of the committee that developed *From Age to Age: The Challenge of Worship with Adolescents*. She is the author of many books for teens and the adults who minister to them.

Introduction

History of the Project

This workshop was first developed in Nebraska in 1993 to involve young people in the effort to make liturgy more "youth-friendly." In my parish I found that liturgists and priests take youth feedback more seriously when the young people are well grounded in some basic principles of liturgy, so I created a workshop to train young people in basic liturgical principles.

The content was revised in Milwaukee in 1998 to be a youth-led workshop. I learned that when teenagers are trained to present a workshop to others, the teen presenters really learn the topic well. In addition, when adults are in the audience, they begin to view young people as leaders of today's church who are excited about their faith.

In 1999 this youth-led workshop became part of "Tomorrow's Present," a youth leadership training project funded by a Lilly grant and developed in the Archdiocese of Milwaukee. This article contains the workshop outline developed for that project. The full version of the project contains additional background material for team formation and a training video. **The full version is available from the Office for Schools, Child, and Youth Ministries, Archdiocese of Milwaukee, 1-414-769-3360.**

About This Workshop

This workshop is a tool to help a parish youth leadership team prepare to present a workshop to youth and adult parish members. The workshop is the initial step young people can take in becoming part of the parish conversation on liturgy. It's important for a parish using the workshop to understand what it is designed to do and what it is not designed to do.

The workshop "Youth-Friendly Liturgy" is

- an effort to whet the appetites of young people for involvement in the liturgical life of the parish
- an opportunity for initial youth leadership training in the area of liturgy
- an opportunity for an intergenerational experience of liturgical interest

The workshop "Youth-Friendly Liturgy" is not

- a complete catechesis on the Eucharist
- a how-to for liturgy

- a program that can be given to youth without liturgical formation of the leadership team

Youth-Friendly Liturgy

Youth-friendly liturgy is a term that can easily be misinterpreted and thus must be used with some caution. This workshop does not suggest that a parish create one Mass on Sunday that is just for young people. Being exclusive is never an indication of good liturgy. Actually, any liturgy that is "youth-friendly" is also "adult-friendly" and "child-friendly." The same principles of good liturgy apply to people of all ages.

Young people like the term *youth-friendly* and often use it to describe liturgy that speaks to real life and is vibrant and welcoming. The term is probably borrowed from the high-tech world that describes "user-friendly computer software" as software that a nonexpert can easily use. Because young people use the term spontaneously, and because this workshop is presented by teens so that more teens might begin to view worship as something significant in their lives, the term *youth-friendly liturgy* is used in this workshop outline.

Who Is the Intended Audience for This Workshop?

The workshop was written for quite a span of ages and backgrounds, including middle school youth, high school youth, and even adults. Those who are younger need background in basic principles of liturgy presented in an engaging, youth-friendly way by high school youth, whom they admire. Adults, who are more advanced than the youth presenters in their understanding of liturgy, still benefit from seeing the exuberance of the young presenters. High school students need to see their peers involved in church leadership. Even younger siblings, brought by the parents of the teen presenters, have enjoyed this workshop and learned some liturgical concepts. A multigenerational crowd can learn from and enjoy this experience together.

Workshop Preparation

Before you actually start training a leadership team of young people, you need to make some preparations. Here are two tools to help you organize: (1) an advance preparation checklist and (2) a workshop supply list.

Advance Preparation Checklist

- ☐ Get support from adult parishioners and parish staff members.
- ☐ Arrange for a time and space to hold the training. It's a good idea to hold the training in a retreat setting, which requires an overnight stay. This training is a lot of work, so scheduling a two- or even three-day event removes some of the pressure of having to cram it all into one day.
- ☐ Go through the supply list thoroughly and note which items have to be gathered, made, or bought. Then gather, buy, and make all supplies; label and box them together.
- ☐ Make copies of the workshop script and put each copy in a binder or folder so that everyone on the team can make notes on their own personal copy.
- ☐ Hold the workshop training event for the team.
- ☐ Have a dress rehearsal of the workshop with parents and siblings of the youth team members and the parish staff. Follow with a potluck meal to celebrate the team's progress. Invite your pastor, liturgist, and other parish staff members to give feedback. Arrange for a parishioner to videotape the rehearsal so that the teen presenters can critique their own performances. Ask a different parishioner to take still photographs, which can be used later for posters and bulletin board notices.
- ☐ Schedule the workshops into the parish calendar.
- ☐ Advertise each workshop with parish bulletin announcements, parish newsletter articles, posters, and letters of invitation to all parish organizations, including youth organizations.
- ☐ If possible, arrange for young people to make an announcement to the assembly at all Masses the weekend before the first workshop is held. A 2-minute commercial from a young person can have a big impact.
- ☐ Schedule a final practice before the first workshop, to be sure that the young people are ready to go.

Workshop Supply List

Part 1

Section A: Welcome
- ☐ resource A, "Section Leaders" (found at the end of the workshop plan)
- ☐ name tags for all participants and workshop presenters
- ☐ chairs for all participants

Section B: Opening Prayer
- [ ] a small prayer table (the size of a piano bench, with the following items on it; hereafter referred to simply as the prayer table):
  - [ ] a tablecloth
  - [ ] a large candle and matches
  - [ ] a large Bible on a Bible stand
  - [ ] an incense bowl with sand in the bottom, charcoal, incense granules (borrow from the parish sacristy)

Section C: Review of Opening Prayer
- [ ] *optional:* a basket of individually wrapped candies
- [ ] poster 1, "The Four Movements of Prayer" (see the appendix on page 207, "Poster Guides," for a sample of this poster) and tape or poster putty

Section D: Symbol Activity
- [ ] liturgy symbol cards (see section D for instructions on preparing these cards)

Section E: Break
- [ ] snacks and drinks
- [ ] plates, cups, napkins

Part 2

Section F: Four Basic Principles of the Liturgy
- [ ] the prayer table
- [ ] an empty plate and a glass goblet (on the prayer table)
- [ ] chairs for all participants (rearranged in auditorium style)
- [ ] a book of Vatican Council II documents or liturgy documents
- [ ] posters 2–8 (see the appendix, "Poster Guides," on pages 207–208 for samples of these posters) and tape or poster putty
- [ ] a sign that says "Applause"
- [ ] markers and four index cards or blank sheets of paper
- [ ] a broad-tip marker to use as a microphone

Section G: Seven Posters and Feedback
- [ ] posters 9–15 (see the appendix, "Poster Guides," on pages 209–210 for samples of these posters) and masking tape or poster putty
- [ ] handout G–1, "In the Heart of the Liturgy" (included at the end of the workshop plan)

Section H: Wrap-Up
☐ one copy of *From Age to Age: The Challenge of Worship with Adolescents*
☐ one copy of handout H–1, "Eight Principles for Vibrant Worship," for each person
☐ *optional:* one copy of handout H–2, "Closing Litany," for each person

Youth-Friendly Liturgy: The Workshop

The workshop is divided into two parts, separated by a break. Within the workshop there are seven separate sections of activities. Each section begins with a brief description, identifies the team roles required, and then gives a script and directions for the presentations and activities in that section.

The team presenting the workshop could be as few as four or five young people, or it could be as large as twenty-five if you assigned a different person to each role. To help you keep track of the team assignments, use resource A, "Section Leaders," included at the end of the workshop plan.

This workshop plan contains detailed directions and a complete script of everything the team needs to say or do for the two-hour workshop. This is helpful for young people who have never led a workshop before. As they become proficient, they can adapt what is here. Just be sure that the theological teaching stays intact.

Part 1

Section A: Welcome (10 minutes)

In this section the team establishes a comfortable rapport with the participants and gives them an overview of what to expect from the workshop.

As the participants gather, ask them to fill out a name tag and then take a seat in the semicircle.

LEADER: _____

LEADER: We're so glad to be here. Thank you all for coming. We're really happy that our parish has begun this youth-friendly liturgy effort. My name is _____, and here's our team: *[The team lines up and each person states his or her name, age or grade, school or parish, and whatever else he or she wishes to add.]*

The purpose of this workshop is to help all of us learn more about liturgy in a meaningful way. It will consist of a variety of activities. In a moment we will begin with a brief prayer service. During the prayer several of you will be invited to come forward and place a small grain of incense on some hot coals. Then a member of our team will make the sign of the cross over us all with the incense.

[Next, the LEADER introduces the PRAYER PRESIDER.]

Section B: Opening Prayer (10 minutes)

The purpose of this section is to celebrate prayer together in a meaningful way.

Advance Preparation

Arrange the chairs in a semicircle. Place a small prayer table in the center. On the prayer table arrange a cloth, a large candle, matches, a Bible on a Bible stand (opened to Psalm 141, with verses 1 and 2 clearly marked), and an incense bowl with sand in the bottom and charcoal on top of the sand. Place the incense granules in a small dish nearby.

Invite a volunteer to do the Scripture reading, Psalm 141:1–2.

Also invite a few volunteers to represent the group by putting incense on the charcoal at the appropriate time.

PRAYER PRESIDER: _____

INCENSE PERSON: _____

1. Call to Prayer: Candlelighting and Greeting

The PRESIDER lights the candle and the charcoal in the incense bowl.

PRESIDER: We begin our prayer together
 in the name of the Father,
 and of the Son,
 and of the Holy Spirit. *[Everyone makes the sign of the cross.]*
  [The PRESIDER looks upward, not making eye contact with the group.] Loving God, we gather so that our prayers to you might be like the rising of sweet-smelling incense. We ask for your grace and help during our time together. Strengthen us in your knowledge and love. We ask this through Christ our Lord. Amen.

2. The Word: Psalm 141

The PRESIDER gestures for the appointed reader to come up and read from the Bible.

READER: A reading from the Book of Psalms *[reading from the Bible]*:
 I call upon you, O Lord, come quickly to me;
  give ear to my voice when I call to you.
 Let my prayer be counted as incense before you,
  and the lifting up of my hands as an evening sacrifice.
 The Word of the Lord.

ALL: Thanks be to God.

3. Response: Incense Ritual

The PRESIDER places a grain of incense on the coals, then gestures for designated members of the assembly to come forward. (A team member could lead the way to make it easier for others to follow the example.) Each person picks up a few granules of incense and reverently drops them on the hot coals before returning to his or her seat.

The INCENSE PERSON picks up the bowl of incense and stands before the assembly, holding the bowl high. (The sand should prevent the bottom of the bowl from becoming too hot.) The PRESIDER motions for the assembly to stand, and the assembly stands. The INCENSE PERSON bows to the people, and the assembly (again following the lead of team members) bows in return. Then the INCENSE PERSON uses the incense to make the sign of the cross over the assembly three times. This is done by first stepping to one side to do that area of the group, then gracefully moving back to the middle to do that area of the group, and finally stepping to the other side to do the last area. Then the INCENSE PERSON returns the bowl to the prayer table.

4. Sending Forth: Blessing

The PRESIDER walks to the front of the assembly and offers this final blessing:

PRESIDER: Loving Creator,
   as we come together to learn more about liturgy,
   [holding hands outward, palms facing down, in a blessing gesture over the assembly]
   bless us with your Spirit of knowledge,
   so that we may grow in every good work we do.
   We ask this through Christ our Lord.
   Amen. *[The PRESIDER blows out candle and then sits down.]*

Section C: Review of Opening Prayer (10 minutes)

In this section the group reflects on the opening prayer experience as a foundation from which to explore the general parts of prayer and then the parts of the Mass.

LEADER: _____

POSTER HOLDER: _____

The LEADER begins by thanking the PRAYER PRESIDER. Then, as an option, the LEADER may get out a basket of individually wrapped candies to be awarded to anyone who answers one of the questions in this section. The candy has worked well as an icebreaker with youth, especially groups that include middle school youth. However, be sensitive to your audience; some have not been entirely comfortable with the candy reinforcement. If the candy is tossed to the recipient, it can feel too much like an animal being thrown food as a reward for doing tricks.

LEADER: Let's talk about prayer. *[The LEADER proceeds to ask some general questions of the group, trying to get them to reflect on the overall experience of prayer. The LEADER uses questions such as those listed below and then continues on to the four movements of prayer.]*

- What did you think was the most engaging part of the opening prayer?
- What did you think were the most important parts of the prayer?
- Did any aspects of this experience seem different or unique? If so, which aspects?

Formal prayer is divided into four basic parts. We sometimes call these four parts the four movements of prayer. Let's see if you can figure out what these four movements are.

How did you know the prayer had started? *[The LEADER touches or holds up the candle and encourages an answer such as, "The candle was lit."]*

Good. This is called the Call to Prayer, or the Gathering, the first movement of prayer.

What was done next? *[The LEADER touches or holds up the Bible and encourages answers such as, "Someone read from the Bible."]*

Right. This is called the Reading, or the Word, the second movement of prayer.

What else happened? *[The LEADER touches the incense bowl and encourages answers such as, "We put grains of incense on the hot coals." Or, "We made the incense smoke."]*

Yes. This is called the Ritual, or the Response, the third movement of prayer.

What happened after that? *[The LEADER holds up his or her hands in the blessing gesture and encourages answers such as, "We prayed the final blessing."]*

Correct. This is called the Blessing, or the Sending Forth, the fourth and last movement of prayer.

So prayer has these four movements:
- the Call to Prayer, or the Gathering [touches the candle]
- the Reading, or the Word [touches the Bible]
- the Ritual, or the Response [touches incense bowl]
- the Blessing, or the Sending Forth [holds hands up in blessing]

We just prayed a short prayer so that you could clearly see the four movements. But usually the four movements are not celebrated in such a simple way. There are movements within the movements.

At Mass the two main parts are called the liturgy of the word and the liturgy of the Eucharist. It is during the liturgy of the word that God speaks to us, the assembly, in the Scriptures proclaimed. We listen to the stories of God's people in history, and through the homily we connect our own life experiences with the biblical stories of God's people.

It is during the liturgy of the Eucharist that we prepare the table and pray the eucharistic prayer, the highest point of the Mass. We also pray the Lord's Prayer and then receive the body and blood of Christ during the Communion Rite. We break bread together because that's what Jesus did at the Last Supper.

[The POSTER HOLDER comes out, holding poster 1, "The Four Movements of Prayer." The LEADER goes to poster 1.] So when we pray at Mass, the overall structure is the same as our opening prayer today, but there are a lot more parts.

[Pointing to the first movement on the poster] The introductory rites could be seen as the first movement. We gather and sing. As an assembly we are the Body of Christ, united for worship. We are greeted, and we pray the opening prayer. How many of you remember the phrase, "Lord have mercy, Christ have mercy?" You are remembering part of the introductory rites.

[Pointing to the second movement on the poster] The second movement takes place during the liturgy of the word. We listen to the first reading, usually from the Old Testament, and we sing a psalm response. Then we listen to the second reading, usually from one of the letters of the New Testament. Next, we sing the Alleluia and listen to the proclamation of the Gospel. Then we listen to the homily, sometimes pray the Nicene Creed, and end with the prayers of the faithful.

How many of you remember these phrases: "The Word of the Lord" and "Thanks be to God"? You are remembering part of the liturgy of the word.

[Pointing to the third movement on the poster] The third movement takes place during the liturgy of the Eucharist. We bring up the gifts and prepare the altar. We pray the eucharistic prayer. How many of you remember these sayings: "Holy, Holy, Holy" and "Christ has died, Christ is risen, Christ will come again" and "Amen, Amen, Amen"? You are remembering the acclamations of the eucharistic prayer. Then we pray the Lord's Prayer, and we receive the body and blood of Christ. All these important things happen during the liturgy of the Eucharist.

[Pointing to the fourth movement on the poster] The concluding rites can be seen as the fourth movement. We are dismissed to go forth "in peace to love and serve God." How many of you remember those words? They are the words from the concluding rites. We sing and we process out of the church. *[The POSTER HOLDER puts the poster up on the wall.]*

So the next time you attend Mass, try to pay attention and see if you can pick out the different movements we just talked about. Remember that the Mass doesn't just have four simple movements. Each of the movements includes many different rituals and responses. Both the liturgy of the word and the liturgy of the Eucharist have movements and even submovements happening within them. The more we learn about the Mass, the more we understand, and the more we can participate.

Section D: Symbol Activity (15 minutes)

This activity helps the participants see that the symbols of liturgy are the symbols of our lives and the symbols of salvation history.

Advance Preparation

Use colored index cards to prepare three sets of liturgy cards. Use a different color of card for each set. That way you will always know to which set a stray card belongs. Simply write one of the following phrases on each index card of a set. Or you can type them onto labels and then peel the labels off and stick them to index cards.

Set 1
Telling good news
People gathering together

Being commissioned or sent
Standing to show respect
Responding to God's call
Saying "Amen," "Yes, I agree," "I promise," or "I do"
Life after death
Setting the table
Remembering special days and anniversaries
Special clothes
Bread
Walking, processing, parading
Giving thanks and praise

Set 2
Saying you are sorry
Listening to the word
Singing and making music
Holding hands
Plants, flowers, leaves
A letter from someone who cares about you
Bringing gifts for the poor
Lighting a candle or candles
Special colors with special symbolic meanings
Light
Wine
People greeting one another
Being sent to do something significant

Set 3
Table
Sharing a meal
Silence
Listening to a story
Oils
Remembering and praying for someone in need
Ashes
Water
Hugs and handshakes
Darkness
Crucifix
Telling stories

LEADER: _____

LEADER: We just learned about the different movements of formal prayer. This is the structure of the liturgy. Now we are going to learn about some symbols of the liturgy.

We will be doing a symbol activity in small groups. Each group will have a set of these liturgy symbol cards. *[The LEADER holds up one pack of cards.]*

One of our team members will guide you through it. It goes like this: We will begin by sharing our names to help the team get to know who you are and help you get to know who we are.

The first person repeats his or her name, picks a card, and reads it. Let's say the card says "water." The person then thinks of how that symbol (water in our example) is a part of his or her own life. This is the first question: How is this symbol part of my life?

Let's pretend that I am a member of your small group. So what are some of the ways that I use water in my life? I would say something like this, "I use water when I shower; I drink water; I swim in water; and I water my plants."

Then everyone else in the group will think of all the ways that symbol (water in our example) is used in the liturgy. This is the second question: How is this symbol used in the liturgy?

Again, let's pretend that I am a member of your small group. So what are some ways we use water in the liturgy? *[The LEADER encourages answers from the participants such as Baptisms, sprinkling rites during the Easter season, or blessing yourself when you come into the church.]*

Good answers. After brainstorming answers to the second question, the next person picks a card and the process begins again. Are there any questions about how to do the activity? This activity will last 10 minutes.

The LEADER has the group count off to form small groups. Then everyone is invited to move their chairs, form small circles, and begin.

At least one team member should join every small group. The team members need to keep things moving and ensure that the whole small group is involved in answering the second question: How is this symbol used in the liturgy? Also the team members need to make sure that everyone in a small group is seated on the same level: either everyone is in a chair or everyone is on the floor.

The LEADER gives everyone a 5-minute warning once 5 minutes have passed, which means half the small group should be finished sharing. After 10 minutes the LEADER calls everyone back together.

LEADER: Who can tell me why we would spend time doing an activity like this? *[The LEADER looks for and encourages any answers such as these:*
- *to learn how the symbols of liturgy relate to our everyday lives and how they are important*
- *to become more familiar with the symbols of liturgy*
- *to get to know one another better]*

Great answers. The more we understand symbols, the more we understand liturgy and the stories of our faith. For example, the sprinkling rite at Mass isn't meant to help us remember drinking water or taking showers at home. It reminds us of Moses parting the Red Sea, and of the baptism of Jesus. It reminds us of our own Baptism, our dying to sin and rising to new life with Christ. We hope that you will start noticing the symbols at Mass and begin thinking of the stories from the Scriptures that make those symbols meaningful.

Section E: Break (15 minutes)

The LEADER from section D announces a 15-minute break, reminding the participants that there is food and drink available.

The team rearranges the chairs for part 2 of the workshop.

Part 2

Section F: Four Basic Principles of the Liturgy (30 minutes)

This section introduces the participants to some shared terms and basic concepts from *The Constitution on the Sacred Liturgy*.

Advance Preparation

During break place the small prayer table on top of a large table, in the front of the room. Arrange the participants' chairs in auditorium style, rows facing the front, with a center aisle. Set up two chairs in the middle of the front of the room, facing the participants. These two chairs are empty. Place a podium off to one side. Set up two more chairs off to the other side, facing the participants. Invite two adults to sit in the two chairs that are off to the side.

LEADER: _____

APPLAUSE SIGN HOLDER: _____

LEADER: Welcome to part 2 of our workshop! Don't worry about writing down the information we'll be teaching you next. Everything will be outlined on a handout we'll give you later. *[The LEADER picks up the book of liturgical documents (or Vatican Council II documents) and flips through the book in an exaggerated fashion.]* Our team had two ideas about how to teach this segment of the workshop. The first idea was to read sections of this book of liturgical documents to you and then give you a test to see how much you learned. *[Other seated team members mumble in loud voices, "Boring!" "Yuck!" "No!"]*

The second idea was to act out in skits four principles of the liturgy and see if you can guess what they are all about. *[Other seated team members cheer "Yeah!" "All right!" "Whoo-whoo!"]* Because we thought the second idea would be more effective, that's what we'll do.

We will be showing you skits about four of the most basic principles of the liturgy as written in *The Constitution on the Sacred Liturgy,* which we call *CSL* for short. *CSL* is one of the sixteen documents of Vatican Council II. And what does *CSL* stand for? *[It is hoped that the group will respond together, "Constitution on the Sacred Liturgy." If they don't, perhaps one or two individuals will raise their hand to answer the question.]*

[Next, The LEADER holds up poster 2, "Constitution on the Sacred Liturgy" and introduces the team members doing the first demonstration.]

Let's have some applause. *[The APPLAUSE SIGN HOLDER holds up the applause sign. The LEADER claps along, then hangs up poster 2.]*

First Demonstration

NARRATOR 1: _____

PLAYER 1–A: _____

PLAYER 1–B: _____

NARRATOR 1: This activity involves two skits. Your job as the audience is to figure out the main difference between the behavior of people in the first skit and the behavior of people in the second skit. If you figure it out, then you will know the first principle of liturgy we'll be talking about today.

Here's the scene: Two people are involved in a ferocious video game. *[PLAYER 1–A and PLAYER 1–B are sitting in chairs, leaning forward, shouting to each other, commenting on the play, and putting everything they have into this ferocious, make-believe video game contest.]*

[The APPLAUSE SIGN HOLDER holds up the applause sign.]

Now you will see these same two people sitting at Mass listening to a homily. *[PLAYER 1–A and PLAYER 1–B are sitting in chairs, looking around, checking their watches, yawning, rolling their eyes, frowning, and looking very uncomfortable.]*

[The APPLAUSE SIGN HOLDER holds up the applause sign.]

What is the critical difference between the behavior of these people in the two skits? *[The NARRATOR encourages the observation that in the first skit, the players were really "into it," but in the second skit they weren't paying attention and didn't care. As soon as anyone says anything even remotely similar to that, the NARRATOR affirms that and goes on to explain the principle.]*

Involvement. That's the principle being demonstrated. *[The LEADER holds up poster 3 and then hangs it on the wall.]* Paragraph 14 of *CSL* talks about the "full, conscious, and active participation . . . called for by the very nature of the Liturgy." *Liturgy* is a Greek word, meaning "the work of the people." So if we are not actively involved at Mass, we can't call it liturgy because liturgy by definition means we are involved, we are participating.

One way we can be involved is by taking part in some of the liturgical ministries. The Mass offers opportunities for us to play an instrument, proclaim one of the readings, bring up the gifts, or distribute Communion. We could also become involved ahead of time by helping to prepare the worship environment or by planning which songs will be sung.

The most important way to be involved is internally, not externally. That means when it's time to sing, we sing. When it's time to pray, we pray. When it's time to listen, we pay attention. We could even look up the readings for Mass ahead of time and see what they are about. We could use those Scripture readings in our personal prayer during the week. We could think about how God is working in the readings and how God is doing that same work today in our own life.

Many teenagers don't know that most parish bulletins list the upcoming readings for the following Sunday. In fact, the U.S. Catholic bishops even list them on their web site at *www.nccbuscc.org*. If you know how to get into your own diocesan web site, there is usually a link to this web site.

[The LEADER thanks the team members who did the first demonstration and asks for some applause. The APPLAUSE SIGN HOLDER holds up the applause sign, and the LEADER claps along. Then the LEADER introduces the team members who will perform the second demonstration.]

Second Demonstration

NARRATOR 2: _____

PLAYER 2–A: _____

PLAYER 2–B: _____

NARRATOR 2: This demonstration also involves two skits. Once again your job as the audience is to figure out the main difference between the people's behavior in the first skit and their behavior in the second skit. If you figure it out, then you will know the second principle of liturgy we'll be looking at today.

Here's the scene: Two teenagers are watching a basketball game. It's almost over. Their team is behind by two points. A second before the buzzer goes off, one of the players from their school attempts a three-pointer. They watch, the ball rolls around the rim, and it . . . GOES IN! Let's see how they react. *[PLAYER 2–A and PLAYER 2–B watch, biting their fingers, clenching their fists, folding their hands, saying, "Please, please, please!" Finally, they jump up and shout, "We won! We won!" and they do high fives and jump up and down and cheer and hug each other.]*

[The APPLAUSE SIGN HOLDER holds up the applause sign. The NARRATOR claps along.]

Now you will see these same two teenagers at Mass, praying the Lord's Prayer. Although it's not an official gesture of the Mass, some people nearby spontaneously start holding hands. Soon the whole row is holding hands, whether they know one another or not. These teens don't know what else to do. We will join them right at the end of the prayer. *[PLAYER 2–A and PLAYER 2–B are standing as far apart as they can, looking in opposite directions as they hold hands, with their hands held up high in the air. They are grimacing and frowning and are visibly uncomfortable as they say in unison, "For the Kingdom, the power, and the glory are yours, now and forever, Amen." At the word "Amen," they pull their hands back, cross their arms or put their hands in their pockets, and stand with their backs to each other, rolling their eyes and looking around.]*

[The APPLAUSE SIGN HOLDER holds up the applause sign. The NARRATOR claps along.]

What is the critical difference between the behavior of these people in the two skits? *[The NARRATOR encourages answers observing that in the first skit the people were excited and weren't afraid to touch and hug. Their unity was obvious. In the second skit, they didn't want to hold hands. They didn't even seem to want to say the words of the prayer together. They were trying to stay apart and detached.]*

[As soon as anyone says anything even remotely similar to that, or if time is really dragging, the NARRATOR affirms the answers made and goes on to explain the principle.]

Public celebration, not a private function. That's the principle here. *[The LEADER holds up poster 4 and hangs it on the wall.]* How do people show unity during a public celebration? What does it look like? Usually they are comfortable with group gestures and rituals. Sports fans united by team enthusiasm will give one another high fives, participate in group cheers, and do the wave. They will often hug after a crucial play or a victory. These expressions of team support are part of what it means to be a fan. However, someone who is dragged to a sporting event and doesn't care about the team and doesn't want to be there will probably not yell the team cheers, do the high fives, or join in the wave. People in that situation will probably want to just keep to themselves and stay private. They won't want to relate to others as community.

At the liturgy, we are community. We are the Body of Christ. You can see our unity by the way we pray together during the rituals of the Mass. We say prayers and responses together. We sing songs and acclamations together. We make certain gestures together—like the sign of the cross and standing to hear the Gospel. This is the way we celebrate.

So unity is the principle being demonstrated. Paragraph 26 of *CSL* says, "Liturgical services are not private functions, but are celebrations belonging to the Church." Now I know that some of you *might* be thinking, "I've been to Mass at some churches. I know what a celebration is, and that's not it!" Well, there are different kinds of celebrations. A couple's romantic anniversary dinner, an active seven-year-old's birthday party, a sports team's victory, and a somber funeral are all different forms of celebration. And when liturgy is done well, it is truly a celebration! We celebrate that Jesus lived, died, and then rose from the dead. We celebrate the love of the Last Supper. We celebrate that we too will rise again after we die. We celebrate our faith community being together. What an amazing thing!

But think about what happens when people don't fully understand the communal nature of the liturgy. They can end up just sitting back and daydreaming or trying to have a private experience with God during the liturgy. But liturgy is not a spectator sport. We are not watching it happen. We *are* it happening.

Watching basketball is a spectator sport. We are watching the game. We are not playing it. Yet when that basketball goes through the hoop, we say, "We won! We won!" We don't say, "Hey, look! Those guys won!" Yet in reality we *aren't even playing the game*. We are just *watching* it. We need to recognize the excitement we have for sports and cultivate that same excitement in our worship.

[The LEADER thanks the team members who did the second demonstration and calls for some applause. The APPLAUSE SIGN HOLDER holds up the applause sign. Then the LEADER introduces the team members for the third demonstration.]

Third Demonstration

Advance preparation. Write each of the following stanzas on a separate index card or sheet of paper. Give the first stanza to PLAYER 3–A and the second stanza to PLAYER 3–B.

Reading is good
if it's short
and to the point.

But elaborate demonstrations of extensive vocabulary can unfortunately disguise a paragraph's actual meaning, which frequently inhibits the reader's understanding, and furthermore inevitably prevents complete appreciation of the experience intended by the author.

NARRATOR 3: _____

PLAYER 3–A: _____

PLAYER 3–B: _____

NARRATOR 3: This demonstration involves a choral reading. Our two readers will each read a charming literary selection for your listening pleasure. Once they are finished, I will ask you to figure out the main difference between the first reading and the second. If you figure it out, then you will know the third principle of liturgy we'll be talking about today.

[PLAYER 3–A and PLAYER 3–B stand together, with their notes, looking very serious.]

PLAYER 3–A: Reading is good
 if it's short
 and to the point.

PLAYER 3–B: But elaborate demonstrations of extensive vocabulary can unfortunately disguise a paragraph's actual meaning, which frequently inhibits the reader's understanding, and furthermore inevitably prevents complete appreciation of the experience intended by the author.

[The APPLAUSE SIGN HOLDER holds up the applause sign, and the NARRATOR claps along.]

NARRATOR 3: What is the critical difference between what each of these two people read? *[The NARRATOR encourages answers reflecting that the first reading was understandable and simple, but the second one was confusing and complicated.]*

[As soon as anyone says anything remotely similar to that, the narrator affirms the answer and goes on to explain the principle.]

Simplicity! That's the liturgical principle here. *[The LEADER holds up poster 5 and hangs it on the wall.]* Paragraph 34 of *CSL* says that the "rites should be . . . short, clear, . . . and not require much explanation."

Think of the sign of the cross. It's so simple. Even a child can learn it. In fact, many children begin to imitate it long before anyone has explained it or taught them how to do it. But as children grow, they begin to understand the deeper meaning of the symbol. They first begin to understand the words, "In the name of the Father, the Son, and the Holy Spirit, amen." Those words tell about the Trinity, the one God in three divine persons.

Next, perhaps children begin to realize the significance of the sign of the cross they make with their hands. Jesus died on a cross. We are asked to take up our cross and follow him. After dying, Christ rose from the dead and will come again at the end of time.

Next, perhaps they will begin to realize that making the cross over themselves is a blessing. They will begin to notice that priests make the same sign when they bless people and special objects.

As they get even older, these young adults may begin to ponder the mystery of the cross that casts its shadow over our life. Blessing ourselves with the sign of the cross doesn't mean that we will never suffer because God is protecting us, but rather that we are blessed in the tradition of the paschal mystery. We too will rise after our death. We too will have pain and doubts and Good Friday moments. We too will be carried through Holy Saturday waiting periods. We too will be raised to Easter Sunday glory. This is our faith. This is the sign of the cross. This is what it means to follow Jesus as a disciple. This is what it means to be a Christian.

All of that—with just this *[demonstrates again the sign of the cross]*. Noble simplicity. As we grow in wisdom and in faith, we begin to understand more deeply the mystery of all that is God and all that is love.

Liturgy done well doesn't mean: "Bring in the circus! Let's entertain these folks! Let's pull out all the stops!" Liturgy done well means noble simplicity. The symbols speak for themselves. Thus something is not right if a parish community goes to Mass on Sunday and often says, "Huh? I don't get it!" We need to find a way to the noble simplicity of sacred liturgy. The symbols must be understood, the readings must be proclaimed well, the homily must speak to our experience, and we must be able to see how the entire liturgy connects to our life. It must connect in a simple but profound way.

[The LEADER thanks the team members who did the third demonstration and calls for some applause. The APPLAUSE SIGN HOLDER holds up the applause sign, and the LEADER claps along. Then the LEADER introduces the team members for the fourth demonstration.]

Fourth Demonstration

NARRATOR 4: _____
PLAYER 4–A: _____
PLAYER 4–B: _____
PLAYER 4–C: _____
PLAYER 4–D: _____

Note: None of the players in this fourth demonstration can be males with long hair. Also, two of the players must bring up chairs, since there are only two set up.

NARRATOR 4: This presentation will be a little different. It will involve all of you, the studio audience. Our gathering will become a talk show, and I will be the talk show host. The topic of our talk show will be, "What is it like to be a guy with long hair?"

Let's see what our special panel of experts says about guys with long hair. And we'll start with you. What's your name, and what do you do?

PLAYER 4–A: My name is _____, and I'm a high school teacher.

NARRATOR 4: And what is it like to be a guy with long hair?

PLAYER 4–A: Well, I knew a teacher who once had a guy with long hair in her class. She told me he always got A's and asked great questions in class. I suppose guys with long hair are smart and like learning.

NARRATOR 4: Thank you. *[To the next panelist:]* And what's your name, and what do you do?

PLAYER 4–B: My name is _____, and I'm a mechanical engineer.

NARRATOR 4: And what is it like to be a guy with long hair?

PLAYER 4–B: Well, I lived next door to a family with a member who had long hair. I saw him take the garbage out every single week. I imagine guys with long hair are neat, tidy, and very dependable.

NARRATOR 4: Thank you. *[To the next panelist:]* What's your name, and what do you do?

PLAYER 4–C: My name is _____, and I'm a doctor.

NARRATOR 4: And what is it like to be a guy with long hair?

PLAYER 4–C: Let's see. I go to church each Sunday, and I like sitting in the same pew. I always notice this guy with long hair sitting toward the front of the church. He's always there, praying. No matter how early I come, he's always there first, already praying. I suspect guys with long hair are very religious, very spiritual people.

NARRATOR 4: Thank you. *[To the next panelist:]* What's your name, and what do you do?

PLAYER 4–D: My name is _____, and I'm a lawyer.

NARRATOR 4: And what is it like to be a guy with long hair?

PLAYER 4–D: My cousin married a guy with long hair. He is really involved in the arts. He sings and dances and acts, and even plays a musical instrument. It's my opinion that guys with long hair are very creative and artistic.

NARRATOR 4: *[To the panelists on the talk show]* Thank you all very much.

[To the group as a whole] So then, according to our panel of experts, it's quite easy to understand what it's like to be a guy with long hair. If you are a guy with long hair, that means you are intellectual, you are clean and tidy, you are deeply religious, and you are creative and artistic.

Ladies and gentlemen, let's take a poll by a show of hands: How many of you agree with our panel of experts? *[The participants may or may not raise their hands.]* How many of you disagree with our panel of experts? *[The participants may or may not raise their hands.]*

What's wrong with this picture? Can anyone tell me why this is a very strange way to run a talk show? *[The NARRATOR encourages answers such as these: "You didn't even ask a guy with long hair," "Guys with long hair were completely left out," or "You didn't include guys with long hair in the conversation."]*

[As soon as anyone says anything similar to that, the NARRATOR affirms that answer and goes on to explain the principle.]

Being inclusive and representative is the principle here! *[The LEADER holds up poster 6 and hangs it on the wall.]* It's the last principle we will be talking about in our workshop. The liturgy needs to be sensitive about including all people of the community. Paragraph 37 of *CSL* says that the "Church respects and fosters the genius and talents of the various races and peoples." And paragraph 38 talks about "adaptations to different groups, regions, and peoples." This means that the presence of young people needs to be reflected, as well as the presence of elderly people, women, people who are deaf, and people who speak different languages.

In other words, if we don't invite everyone into the conversation, we aren't being inclusive. It's not good enough to think we know what it's like to be someone else, or to think we know what another person wants or needs.

[The LEADER thanks the team members who played the panel of experts and calls for some applause. The APPLAUSE SIGN HOLDER holds up the applause sign, and the LEADER claps along. The panel of experts picks up their chairs and goes back to sit with the "audience."]

Part of being inclusive is to deliberately represent diversity in the Mass. If a parish has members from three or four cultures, but all the people on the parish council are from just one of the cultures, then the parish council doesn't represent the diversity of the parish. The same could be said of a parish council that is made up of all men, or of all women, or of only people in their thirties.

So, for example, if a parish is going to have a long-term conversation about youth-friendly liturgy, that means the conversation should include young people. Adults by themselves won't be able to decide what is and isn't "youth-friendly" without first talking with young people. Young people need to take their proper place at the table.

So let's talk about the ways a parish can try to include everyone—not just young people, but everyone. How can different kinds of people be welcomed and included? For example, how could a parish show visitors that they are welcomed? How are they greeted at the door when they first enter? *[The NARRATOR looks for answers like, "people being equally friendly to everyone," "people smiling," and "people calling you by name."]*

How could a parish try to do things so that every age-group feels special and important? *[The NARRATOR looks for answers like, "special celebrations that highlight different events," "including all ages whenever possible in liturgical ministries," and similar ideas.]*

How could a church or parish building demonstrate that a person using a wheelchair is welcome? *[The NARRATOR looks for answers along these lines: "space and ramps for wheelchairs not only in the exits and where the assembly sits but also near the altar so that a person who uses a wheelchair could comfortably proclaim the word and distribute Communion."]*

How might a parish demonstrate that persons who speak different languages are welcome? *[The NARRATOR looks for answers such as "bilingual liturgies and events," "music and customs from different cultures," "sign language interpretation for the deaf," and so on.]*

How might a parish demonstrate inclusiveness to both genders? *[The NARRATOR looks for answers such as, "being sure women are* included in all liturgical ministries," and "using gender-inclusive language."]

So let's keep going. What are some ways a parish might be exclusive? Or what are other ways we have been exclusive in part 2 of our workshop? *[The NARRATOR moves close to the two chairs up front where the adults have been sitting and puts a hand on the back of one of the chairs. The NARRATOR looks for answers noting that some adults are in the "more important area" because it is closer to the front of the room where the prayer table is.]*

[If no one says anything related to that situation, the NARRATOR encourages thinking by asking, "For example, Does it seem as if some participants are more important here?" That usually sparks an answer.]

Even the way the church interior is designed can be exclusive: a long space with all the people facing forward in rows, and the altar way up front. It may make the front seem like the only special area; the rest of the church building may seem insignificant in comparison. No one can see anyone's face—just the backs of people's heads.

Some architects call this kind of space "two-room worship space" because it seems as if the space is divided into two spaces, the holy space and the not-so-holy space. This setup may remind you of a classroom. *[The LEADER holds up poster 7 and hangs it on the wall.]*

Remember the room arrangement we started the workshop with? The prayer table or altar was closer to the people, and everyone could see one another. Look at this space now. *[The NARRATOR pauses and looks around.]* Doesn't it feel different?

When the people surround the altar and can see one another's faces, it's more obvious that all the space is holy space. No one is too far away from the altar. Some architects like to call this "one-room worship space." It is less like a classroom and more like a dining room setup. *[The LEADER holds up poster 8 and hangs it on the wall.]*

[The NARRATOR has the two adults stand up. The NARRATOR then moves the two chairs back to where the people are sitting. The NARRATOR motions for the two adults to sit back down on the chairs. They are now facing front, in the first row, or in the first and second rows.]

Sometimes the presider chair sits in a spot like this, with the people. It's still a special presider chair, and it usually still matches the style of the altar and the ambo. It reminds us of the importance of the priest as presider at the eucharistic assembly. But in an effort to create one-room worship space, it is sometimes placed closer to the chairs of the assembly. That way it reduces the distance between the presider and the assembly; the space is less likely to interfere with communication between the priest and the people.

Let me ask you this: Where is Christ present during the liturgy? There are some obvious answers, but there is one that is usually overlooked. Let's see what you come up with. *[Pause.]* Just call out an answer. *[The NARRATOR allows for all kinds of guesses before revealing the answers. If a participant offers any of the following answers, the NARRATOR affirms the answer and repeats it.]* Christ is present in (1) the eucharistic bread and wine, (2) the presider, (3) the word proclaimed to the assembly, and (4) the assembly gathered.

[If a participant guesses incorrectly (crucifix, holy water, etc.), respond with a comment such as, "Well, that's a very important symbol, but it's not one of the four modes of the real presence of Christ."]

Usually it's the people who are overlooked. It's us! The assembly gathered together! We are the Body of Christ. Liturgy would seem silly without the people. Worship space that allows people to see the faces of other people is helpful. We can be more in touch with that fourth mode of the real presence of Christ—the gathered assembly.

So let's put our space back to the way it was, with the prayer table in the middle and our chairs in a semicircle. Then we'll get on with our next activity. *[The group sets up the space the way it was in part 1. While the furniture is being moved, some team members post on the wall the seven posters that have the seven feedback categories written on them.]*

Section G: Seven Posters and Feedback (20 minutes)

This activity gives youth and adults a chance to discuss different aspects of the liturgy and offer feedback to their parish leadership—affirmation for the ways the liturgy is already inclusive of youth, as well as thoughtful, concrete suggestions on ways the liturgy might be made more youth-friendly. The activity is also meant to raise awareness of the many ways youth can become more involved in what it takes to create a rich celebration of the liturgy.

Note: Because this activity is mostly talking, with limited participant involvement, it is a good idea to have two leaders who alternate speaking.

LEADER G–1: _____

LEADER G–2: _____

LEADER G–1: Here's what we are going to do next. We are going to take everything we have learned from *CSL* and put it here. *[LEADER G–1 holds out one hand.]*

Next, we are going to take everything you know about your own parish and put it here. *[LEADER G–1 holds out the other hand.]*

And then we are going to put it all together! *[Leader G–1 slaps the hands together over his or her head.]*

We're going to put together what you know about your parish with what you know about *CSL*. *[LEADER G–1 has everyone stand up together and do that same exercise, with everyone holding out their hands and slapping them over their head.]* Good job! Sit down for one more minute.

LEADER G–2: Take a look around at the posters. Each one highlights a different aspect of liturgy. We'll mention each poster, one at a time. As we make a few comments about each one, we want you to think about *CSL* in relation to your parish and how things are happening there.

LEADER G–1: Youth involvement in liturgical ministries. *[LEADER G–2 points to poster 9.]* The most important role we have at Mass is to be active participants of the assembly gathered. Besides that important role, what other special roles do youth have during the Mass? Think of your parish and ask yourself these questions: Do young people serve as singers or musicians at Mass? Do young people serve as eucharistic ministers? as altar servers? as ministers of hospitality or ushers? How might your parish involve young people more in these areas?

[Note: The team needs to be mindful of the local practices of each parish and diocese where this workshop is being presented. In some places it is customary for young people to serve as liturgical ministers only after they reach a certain age, are confirmed, receive special training, and so on. It's best to check with your parish contact ahead of time so that this section of the workshop can be presented in the most appropriate manner.]

LEADER G–2: Youth involvement in planning liturgy. *[LEADER G–1 points to poster 10.]* What kinds of things are young people involved with, ahead of time, in preparation for the liturgy? Do teenagers serve on the liturgy committee? Do teenagers help prepare the worship environment—any of the things that improve our ability to pray well and make our worship space look more welcoming for the community, such as arranging flowers and candles, making seasonal changes (for example, different colored altar cloths, banners, etc., for Lent, Easter, Advent, Christmas, Ordinary Time)? How might your parish increase teen involvement in this area?

LEADER G–1: Music. *[LEADER G–2 points to poster 11.]* Does some of the music have a contemporary sound or a youthful spirit? Are opportunities provided for young people to give input regarding musical selections and arrangements? Do young people sing along at Mass? Do the musical groups that lead the singing actually encourage the assembly to sing, or are they more like performers? Do they sing in a way that might actually discourage others from singing?

LEADER G–2: Presider or homilist. *[LEADER G–1 points to poster 12.]* Does preaching connect the Scriptures with real life today? Do the homilies ever mention stories of teenagers? Do young people usually listen to the homilies? Are opportunities provided for young people to talk to the presider or homilist about the stories of the readings and the stories of their own lives?

LEADER G–1: Cultural concerns. *[LEADER G–2 points to poster 13.]* Do the music and prayers reflect a respect for and inclusiveness of people from all over the world? Does the assembly ever sing songs in more than one language? Is it clear that the leadership of the parish reflects a diversity of age, gender, and race? Is there ever sign language interpretation? Are there ramps and ample space for persons who use wheelchairs or walkers? Could a person who doesn't speak English feel welcome? Do people with small children feel welcome? Do the elderly as well as the young feel included?

LEADER G–2: Liturgical catechesis. *[LEADER G–1 points to poster 14.]* Do teenagers generally understand the liturgy? Do they understand the symbols? Do they know what the rituals are all about? Do they get the meaning behind the sacraments? Is there a way for teenagers' questions to be answered?

LEADER G–1: Other. *[LEADER G–2 points to poster 15.]* This is the category for all categories that didn't get their own category. This is the leftovers category. So if you have some feedback in mind that doesn't fit in any of the six categories we mentioned, it goes here.

LEADER G–2: We will soon give you a chance to write down some feedback for your parish. These seven posters will structure your feedback. As you can see, a vertical line has been drawn down the middle of each poster. On one side it says, "Way to go!" and on the other it says, "Why not?"

On the side of the sheet that says, "Way to go!" you will have the opportunity to affirm your parish for the good things that are happening in that area.

On the side of the sheet that says, "Why not?" please take this opportunity to think about what could make liturgy even better in that area.

Notice that there is not a column on these posters for you to write down complaints and criticisms. Our purpose is not to give negative feedback. Instead our purpose is to give positive feedback for areas in which the principles of *CSL* are in place, and to give positive suggestions for ways that our parish could do an even better job.

LEADER G–1: As you write down your comments, keep in mind that what you write should be consistent with the four principles we learned from *CSL*. To make that easier for you, we are going to give you a handout that outlines what we have talked about. So for every comment you write down, we want you to put a number next to it to tell us which of the four principles you were thinking of when you made your comment: (1) involvement, (2) public celebration, (3) simple, and (4) inclusive and representative.

I think an example will help. Let's say someone wanted to write this down: "In the homily, the priest relates stories about the people he lived with in Mexico while learning Spanish. Would this comment go under "Way to Go!" or "Why Not?" *[LEADER G–1 looks for and encourages the answer, "Way to Go!"]* Which newsprint would one write this on? *[LEADER G–1 looks for and encourages the answer, "Presider or homilist," although "Cultural concerns" might also come up as an answer.]* What number principle does this comment reflect? *[LEADER G–1 looks for and encourages the answer "(4) inclusive and representative."]*

LEADER G–2: It might be more productive if you talked in smaller groups of three or four before you write down your comments. That way you can try out your suggestions and be sure that what you say will make sense to all the youth and adults who read them.

After you have finished discussing, proceed as a group to each of the posters and write down your comments. Team members are here to assist you with any questions you might have.

The team members distribute handout G–1, "In the Heart of the Liturgy." The participants walk around, talk, and write on the posters. Team members mingle with the participants to answer questions or to get help from some of the adults if a question is too complicated for them to answer alone. Team members also try to keep the movement going. If large groups are bunched up around one or two of the posters, team members encourage the participants to move on to another category and then come back later.

Section H: Wrap-Up (10 minutes)

LEADER: _____

[The LEADER calls the group back together again.]

LEADER: We want you to know that these four are not the only principles in *CSL*. But they are a good start toward some basic knowledge about the liturgy.

In the summer of 1997, the National Federation for Catholic Youth Ministry published a booklet called *From Age to Age: The Challenge of Worship with Adolescents*. *[The LEADER holds up the booklet.]* It quotes all the major liturgy documents, including *CSL,* and it includes quotes from teenagers as well.

From Age to Age talks about the charisms of young people. A charism is a special gift from God. *From Age to Age* cites eight more principles of vibrant worship with adolescents. Parishes that are serious about youth-friendly liturgy usually benefit from reading this booklet.

On your way out, you can pick up another handout—an outline of those eight principles from *From Age to Age [handout H–1]*.

[The LEADER asks a parish staff person (pastor, liturgist, or other leader) to explain what the parish's next step will be in their process of making their weekly liturgies more youth-friendly. This person comes up, speaks, and answers questions.]

LEADER: I'd like to thank you all once again for coming. We really enjoyed being with you today, and we hope you think it was time well spent. Don't forget to pick up your last handout. It's called "Eight Principles for Vibrant Worship." It outlines information about *From Age to Age:*

The Challenge of Worship with Adolescents. If you have any comments, questions, or suggestions, please feel free to come talk with any of us. Once again, thanks for coming.

Note: If you would prefer to end with a prayer, there is an optional closing litany on handout H–2, "Closing Litany."

Section Leaders

Part 1

Section A: Welcome
LEADER: _____

Section B: Opening Prayer
PRAYER PRESIDER: _____
INCENSE PERSON: _____

Section C: Review of Opening Prayer
LEADER: _____
POSTER HOLDER: _____

Section D: Symbol Activity
LEADER: _____

Part 2

Section F: Four Basic Principles of the Liturgy
LEADER: _____
APPLAUSE SIGN HOLDER: _____
NARRATOR 1: _____
PLAYER 1–A: _____
PLAYER 1–B: _____
NARRATOR 2: _____
PLAYER 2–A: _____
PLAYER 2–B: _____
NARRATOR 3: _____
PLAYER 3–A: _____
PLAYER 3–B: _____
NARRATOR 4: _____
PLAYER 4–A: _____

Resource A: Permission to reproduce this resource for program use is granted.

PLAYER 4–B: _____
PLAYER 4–C: _____
PLAYER 4–D: _____

Section G: Seven Posters and Feedback

LEADER G–1: _____
LEADER G–2: _____

Section H: Wrap-Up

LEADER: _____

In the Heart of the Liturgy

The symbols of liturgy are the symbols of life.	We gather, We share the story, We share the meal, We are sent forth.

Principles from the Constitution on the Sacred Liturgy

1. Involvement

Liturgy demands our involvement. If we aren't involved, then it isn't liturgy. *Liturgy* means "the work of the people."

"full, conscious, and active participation . . . called for by the very nature of the liturgy" (number 14).

2. Public Celebration

Liturgy is a time to celebrate together; it is not a time for individual prayer and devotions.

"Liturgical services are not private functions, but are celebrations belonging to the Church" (number 26).

3. Simple

Liturgy should be easy to understand.

"The rites should be . . . short, clear, . . . and not require much explanation" (number 34).

4. Inclusive

Liturgy includes and respects the cultures of the gathered community.

"The Church respects and fosters the genius and talents of the various races and peoples" (number 37).

". . . adaptations to different groups, regions, and peoples . . ." (number 38).

One-room worship space unites us and encourages public celebration.	Two-room worship space separates us and encourages private prayer.

The most important symbol of Jesus in the liturgy is YOU, the gathered assembly!

Handout G–1: Permission to reproduce this handout for program use is granted.

Eight Principles for Vibrant Worship

1. **Vibrant Worship with adolescents celebrates their involvement in the church's life and mission**

   Parishes and Catholic schools demonstrate this principle by:
   - encouraging youth to join with adults and their peers in activities for service and justice in the larger community;
   - providing opportunities for youth to celebrate liturgy related to service and justice activities;
   - encouraging youth to exercise their natural leadership gifts and talents.

2. **Vibrant worship with adolescents invites and accepts their authentic participation**

   Parishes and Catholic schools demonstrate this principle by:
   - acknowledging youth faith issues at all liturgies in ways appropriate to the rites;
   - training youth as liturgical ministers;
   - scheduling liturgies at youth events prepared with youth;
   - inviting youth to help prepare the community liturgies.

3. **Vibrant worship with adolescents attends to the diversity of ages and cultures in the assembly**

   Parishes and Catholic schools demonstrate this principle by:
   - exploring new music, song texts, and service music being composed for liturgy;
   - inviting youth to act as cultural resources—informing liturgy committees about current "signs of the times" that could be incorporated in the prayers, songs, or rituals;
   - giving youth experiences of other cultural worship styles so that they can gain a greater appreciation of their own.

4. **Vibrant worship with adolescents roots and fosters their personal prayer relationship with God**

   Parishes and Catholic schools demonstrate this principle by:
   - scheduling seasonal prayer events for youth;
   - providing family prayer resources;

- including personal prayer time within all youth events and catechetical sessions.

5. Vibrant worship includes effective preaching of the Word

Parishes and Catholic schools demonstrate this principle by:
- inviting youth to reflect on the seasonal readings and to offer connections to their lives;
- providing regular opportunities for youth to study the Scriptures;
- encouraging those who preach to use current examples and storytelling techniques.

6. Vibrant worship has a youthful spirit in music and song

Parishes and Catholic schools demonstrate this principle by:
- inviting youth to participate in the choirs and musical ensembles;
- exploring contemporary accompaniments and focusing on music's sound and pace;
- expanding the repertoire of hymns and songs to include youth selections.

7. Vibrant worship incorporates visually dynamic symbols and actions

Parishes and Catholic schools demonstrate this principle by:
- inviting youth to assess the visual dynamics of the liturgical rituals and symbols;
- providing visual aids (for example, orders of worship, copies of the readings, and so forth) to encourage youth participation;
- exploring the appropriate use of media at liturgy.

8. Vibrant worship has an interactive and communal dimension

Parishes and Catholic schools demonstrate this principle by:
- focusing on the hospitality provided at liturgy;
- encouraging teens to attend liturgy with their friends;
- building a sense of community among youth before liturgy;
- affirming the presence and involvement of teens whenever possible.

(Adapted from NFCYM, *From Age to Age: The Challenge of Worship with Adolescents,* numbers 48–75)

Closing Litany

ADULTS: Young people, you have energy and spirit.
You have freshness and new ideas.
You are life for the church.

YOUTH: Youth advocates, you have experience and insight.
You have lived through many transitions.
You are wisdom for the church.

ADULTS: Young people, you challenge us.
You urge us to move forward.
Your voice is prophetic.

YOUTH: Youth advocates, you empower us when you listen to us.
You encourage us to grow.
Your voice is our support.

ADULTS: Young people, you are creative and brave.
You ask the questions we have never even considered.
We learn from your honesty.

YOUTH: Youth advocates, you are nurturing and trusting.
You journey with us as we seek the answers together.
We learn from your openness.

ADULTS: Young people, you are the light of the world.
Because of you, we see more clearly.
Our path is illuminated.
What a blessing you are to us!

YOUTH: Youth advocates, you are the salt of the earth.
Because of you, life has more flavor.
Our experiences are richer.
What a blessing you are to us!

BOTH: We thank our Almighty Creator for gifting us with you.
We praise the Master of the Universe
for the challenges we will meet together,
the problems we will solve side by side,
and the lessons we will teach one another.
We ask the Author of Love to shower us with grace
that we might always be dedicated to one another.
We pray in the name of the One who is our God. Amen.

Appendix: Poster Guides

Poster 1:
The Four Movements of Prayer

> The **1st** Movement of Prayer:
> The Call to Prayer
> The Gathering
>
> The **2nd** Movement of Prayer:
> The Reading
> The Word
>
> The **3rd** Movement of Prayer:
> The Ritual
> The Response
>
> The **4th** Movement of Prayer:
> The Blessing
> The Sending Forth

Poster 2:
Constitution on the Sacred Liturgy

> *Constitution on the Sacred Liturgy*

Poster 3:
Involvement

> **INVOLVEMENT**
>
> ". . . full, conscious, and active participation in liturgical celebrations called for by the very nature of the Liturgy"
> (*CSL,* number 14).

Poster 4:
Public Celebration

> **PUBLIC CELEBRATION, NOT PRIVATE FUNCTION**
>
> "Liturgical services are not private functions, but are celebrations belonging to the Church"
> (*CSL,* number 26).

Poster 5:
Simple

> # NOBLE SIMPLICITY
>
> "The rites should be . . . short, clear, . . . and not require much explanation"
> (*CSL,* number 34).

Poster 6:
Inclusive

> # INCLUSIVITY AND REPRESENTATION
>
> "The Church respects and fosters the genius and talents of the various races and peoples"
> (*CSL,* number 37).
>
> ". . . variations and adaptations to different groups, regions, and peoples . . ."
> (*CSL,* number 38).

Poster 7:
Two-Room Worship Space

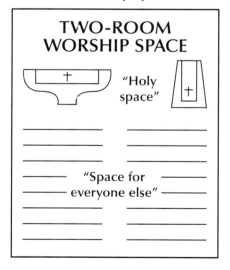

Poster 8:
One-Room Worship Space

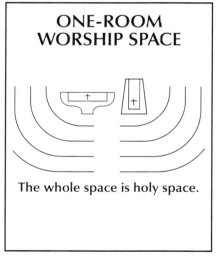

Poster 9: Youth Involvement
in Liturgical Ministries

YOUTH INVOLVEMENT IN LITURGICAL MINISTRIES	
Way to Go!	Why Not?

Poster 10: Youth Involvement
in Planning Liturgy

YOUTH INVOLVEMENT IN PLANNING LITURGY	
Way to Go!	Why Not?

Poster 11:
Music

MUSIC	
Way to Go!	Why Not?

Poster 12:
Presider or Homilist

PRESIDER OR HOMILIST	
Way to Go!	Why Not?

Poster 13:
Cultural Concerns

CULTURAL CONCERNS	
Way to Go!	Why Not?

Poster 14:
Liturgical Catechesis

LITURGICAL CATECHESIS	
Way to Go!	Why Not?

Poster 15:
Other

OTHER	
Way to Go!	Why Not?

Appendix

A Checklist for Fostering Vibrant Worship with Youth

Introduction

This checklist can help you evaluate the youth inclusiveness of your parish or school liturgies. Use it to foster discussion on this topic with your parish or school pastoral team or liturgy team. Better yet, invite a group of parish youth or school students to fill out the checklist and compare their responses to the responses of your liturgy team. Be prepared to help define some of the terms on the checklist for youth who are not familiar with them.

Each area of the checklist is tied to one or more articles in *Vibrant Worship with Youth*. For the areas in which the checklist may indicate that growth is needed in your parish or school, consult the articles listed in that section for further background and ideas. (Note: The articles do not directly address every item on the survey.)

How Youth-Inclusive Are Our Liturgies?

For each of the following items, check the column that most accurately describes how you feel about this aspect of your parish or school liturgies.

Item	This needs growth	We try to do this	We do this well
The Liturgical Environment and the Participation of the Assembly			
1. Our liturgical space allows room for people to gather and mingle before and after the liturgy.	[ ]	[ ]	[ ]
2. Our liturgical space fosters a feeling of participation in our liturgies rather than a feeling of being a spectator.	[ ]	[ ]	[ ]
3. Our entire parish or school community actively participates in all aspects of the liturgy (singing, responding, listening, gesturing, and so on).	[ ]	[ ]	[ ]
4. Our liturgical environment is enhanced with dramatic and powerful liturgical images that speak to young people.	[ ]	[ ]	[ ]
5. In our liturgical celebrations youth feel welcome as valued members of our gathered community.	[ ]	[ ]	[ ]

Articles related to this topic:
- "Ready to Assemble: Youth as Part of the Liturgical Assembly"
- "Youth and Liturgy: There Is Work to Do"

Music

1. We have a liturgical music advisory board or which youth are represented.	[ ]	[ ]	[ ]

Permission to reproduce this handout for program use is granted.

Item	This needs growth	We try to do this	We do this well
2. We use youth-friendly songs in our liturgies—that is, songs with a strong beat and emotive sound that are singable and have lyrics that speak to young people.	[ ]	[ ]	[ ]
3. We have strong musical ensembles that incorporate a variety of instruments and include many voices, including young voices.	[ ]	[ ]	[ ]
4. We apprentice young people into our music ministry to foster their musical talent and ministry calling.	[ ]	[ ]	[ ]

Articles related to this topic:
- "Spirited Music and Singing"
- "Active Teens in Liturgical Ministries—It Can Work"
- "Youth and Liturgy: A Hispanic Perspective"
- "Youth and Liturgy: An African American Perspective"

Liturgy and Catechesis

Item	This needs growth	We try to do this	We do this well
1. Young people in our community understand the meaning of liturgical actions and symbols.	[ ]	[ ]	[ ]
2. We provide opportunities for young people to encounter a variety of worship experiences.	[ ]	[ ]	[ ]
3. We create opportunities for young people to reflect on their experience of liturgy and its role in their spiritual lives.	[ ]	[ ]	[ ]

Articles related to this topic:
- "Liturgical Catechesis: A Parish Workshop Model"
- "Ready to Assemble: Youth as Part of the Liturgical Assembly"

Item	This needs growth	We try to do this	We do this well
Homilies			
1. Homilies are well prepared, passionately delivered, and have depth.	[ ]	[ ]	[ ]
2. Homilies are to the point and not excessively long.	[ ]	[ ]	[ ]
3. Homilies use appropriate stories and examples that connect to young people's lived experience.	[ ]	[ ]	[ ]
4. Homilists sometimes use props or visual aids.	[ ]	[ ]	[ ]
5. Homilists spend time with youth to hear their reflections on the Scriptures.	[ ]	[ ]	[ ]

Articles related to this topic:
- "Ten Things to Keep in Mind When Preaching to Youth"
- "Youth and Liturgy: An African American Perspective"
- "Fostering Vibrant Worship in Catholic Schools"

Item	This needs growth	We try to do this	We do this well
Cultural Inclusiveness			
1. We incorporate symbols, images, and practices that speak to all the cultures represented in our parish or school.	[ ]	[ ]	[ ]
2. Our liturgical music reflects a variety of cultural heritages.	[ ]	[ ]	[ ]
3. We celebrate the religious holidays that are special to the cultural heritages of the many people who make up the church—particularly those in our parish or school.	[ ]	[ ]	[ ]

Articles related to this topic:
- "Vibrant Multicultural Liturgy: Saint Michael's Story"
- "Youth and Liturgy: An African American Perspective"
- "Youth and Liturgy: A Hispanic Perspective"

Item	This needs growth	We try to do this	We do this well
Liturgical Ministries			
1. Youth participate in a variety of liturgical ministries in our regular parish or school worship.	[ ]	[ ]	[ ]
2. Young people are actively recruited to share their gifts in liturgical ministries and feel accepted by the entire parish or school community in doing so.	[ ]	[ ]	[ ]
3. Youth in liturgical ministries receive appropriate training and spiritual formation for their roles.	[ ]	[ ]	[ ]

Articles related to this topic:
- "Active Teens in Liturgical Ministries—It Can Work"
- "Spirited Music and Singing"

Other Issues

Item	This needs growth	We try to do this	We do this well
1. We incorporate liturgical drama into our worship, recognizing the power of sacred drama.	[ ]	[ ]	[ ]
2. Issues and events that affect young people directly are a regular part of the prayers of the faithful and other community prayers.	[ ]	[ ]	[ ]
3. Young people are actively involved in liturgical planning and preparation.	[ ]	[ ]	[ ]
4. We occasionally celebrate important moments in young people's lives—the beginning of school, retreats, Christian service, graduation, and so on—with special youth liturgies.	[ ]	[ ]	[ ]

Articles related to this topic:
- "Training Youth for Liturgical Drama"
- "Fostering Vibrant Worship in Catholic Schools"
- "Youth and Liturgy: There Is Work to Do"

Acknowledgments (*continued*)

The Scripture quotations contained herein are from the New Revised Standard Version of the Bible. Copyright © 1989 by the Division of Christian Education of the National Council of Churches of Christ in the United States of America. All rights reserved.

All the quotations cited as *From Age to Age* are excerpted from *From Age to Age: The Challenge of Worship with Adolescents,* by the National Federation for Catholic Youth Ministry (Washington, D.C.: NFCYM, 1997). Copyright © 1997 by the NFCYM. Used with permission.

The quotation by Pope John Paul II on page 24 is from a prayer vigil on World Youth Day, August 1993.

The quotations on pages 36–37, 40, 57, 74, 79, 85, 185, 188, 189, 192, 207, and 208 are from *The Constitution on the Sacred Liturgy (Sacrosanctum Concilium, 1963)* and the *General Instruction of the Roman Missal,* by Pope Paul VI and the fathers of the Second Vatican Council; English translation copyright © 1982 by the International Committee on English in the Liturgy (ICEL), as quoted in *The Liturgy Documents: A Parish Resource,* third edition, volume 1 (Chicago: Liturgy Training Publications, 1991), numbers 14, 14, 59, 114, 118 and 14, 43, 14, 26, 34, 37 and 38, 14 and 26, and 34, 37, and 38, respectively. Copyright © 1991 by the Archdiocese of Chicago. Used with permission. All rights reserved.

The quote on page 37 is from *General Instruction of the Roman Missal,* number 3, copyright © 1982 by the ICEL, as quoted in *The Liturgy Documents,* volume 1, page 46. Copyright © 1991 by the Archdiocese of Chicago.

The excerpts on pages 48, 50, and 57 are from *Catechism of the Catholic Church,* by the Libreria Editrice Vaticana, translated by the USCC (Washington, D.C.: USCC, 1994), numbers 1074, 1204, and 2629, respectively. Copyright © 1994 by the USCC—Libreria Editrice Vaticana.

The statistic cited on page 48 is from "Catholics Are Confused on the Meaning of Eucharist," by Lee Strong, *The Tablet,* publication of the Diocese of Brooklyn, New York, 26 July 1997, pages 1, 5.

The quote by John Baptist de La Salle on pages 59–60 is from the first point of the fourth meditation, *Meditations* (Landover, Maryland: Lasallian Publications, 1994), page 439. Copyright © 1994 by the Christian Brothers Conference.

The quotations on pages 75 and 80 are taken from *Music in Catholic Worship,* by the United States Catholic Conference (USCC) (Washington, D.C.: USCC, 1983), numbers 17 and 15, as quoted in *The Liturgy Documents,* volume 1, page 279.

The quote on page 154 is from *In Spirit and Truth: Black Catholic Reflections on the Order of Mass,* by the National Conference of Catholic Bishops (NCCB) (Washington, D.C.: USCC, 1988), page 6. Copyright © 1988 by the USCC.

The quote on page 156 is from the back cover of *Plenty Good Room: The Spirit and Truth of African American Worship,* by the USCC (Washington, D.C.: USCC, 1990). Copyright © 1990 by the USCC.